Before and After the Internet

THE MANY FACES OF A
BULLY,
ABUSE,
AND ADDICTION,

We Are Created for Healing and Restoration

GRACE FRANCIS

WESTBOW
PRESS®
A DIVISION OF THOMAS NELSON
& ZONDERVAN

WestBow Press books may be ordered through booksellers or by contacting:

WestBow Press
A Division of Thomas Nelson & Zondervan
1663 Liberty Drive
Bloomington, IN 47403
www.westbowpress.com
844-714-3454

ISBN: 978-1-6642-2675-3 (sc)
ISBN: 978-1-6642-2674-6 (hc)
ISBN: 978-1-6642-2676-0 (e)

Library of Congress Control Number: 2021904612

Print information available on the last page.

WestBow Press rev. date: 04/06/2021

CONTENTS

AUTHOR NOTES

These stories are true to life. However, I have changed the names of all people and places to protect the forgiven. Any and all changes have been made to preserve the anonymity of an individual, whether living or deceased, and their whereabouts, time sequence, and gender identity. Any resemblance in any form is strictly coincidental.

A medical disclaimer applies to any statement or claim made concerning the health benefits of any type of food or suggested dietary changes. The aforementioned is not intended to diagnose, treat, cure, or prevent any disease. The content is not meant to be a substitute for professional medical advice. Always seek the advice of your physician or other qualified professional.

To the Lord Jesus Christ: He is my all in all. And—because of Him—I live.

To my husband, Danny, who has my heart: Thank you for your support throughout this project.

To my grandmother, whom I loved dearly: One day I'll see you in heaven.

To my parents and extended family: I love you all. Thank you for my Christian heritage.

To all my children: I'll love you always and forever.

To every precious woman who has touched my life in unforgettable ways.

To those who have been *bullied in life* by people, abuse, or drugs.

PREFACE

As I was growing up back in the day, the word *bully* was a nominal term; it was almost a nonexistent word. Comparing yesteryear to today, it's become a universal noun, and the meaning has grown exponentially.

Over time, the above meaning of the word *bully* needed to be expanded, and so it was, and so it is here inside this book. Today the labels *bully, bullies,* and *bullying* cover everything from projecting hate to the bully drugs—and, yes, drugs, as you will find out, are also bullies. However, in this broad definition of a bully, there are both chief similarities and differences *before* and *after* the internet and social media networks, but noticeably, the outcome remains the same: broken, hurting, and shattered lives. God is a God of restoration. Candidly, my memory stream of being bullied led to a collection of authentic events, where the names have been changed to protect the forgiven and preserve the dead. Yet how did I overcome and forgive what happened?

Bullying has affected me as well as others. Some call this a bullying epidemic, and others say that a bully is abusive. Plus, abuse is only one attribute of bullying. In this book, you will read about bullies, abusers, and the addict who overcame drugs and more, as well as other true stories. Nonetheless, God wants to heal the whole person: body, mind, and soul. No matter what criteria bullying falls under or how far back an incident occurred, the Lord wants to wipe away our tears. Revelation 7:17 says: "For the Lamb who is in the midst of the throne will shepherd them and lead them to living fountains of waters. And God will wipe away every tear from their eyes."

Years prior, God impressed upon me (really, He told me) to write a book, but on what? For a time, it remained unspoken. There were also others who encouraged me to write a book, but on what? My private secrets, hidden trauma, or personal nightmare? Or was it how I was bullied for being overweight and then for losing the weight or all of it? Then, I wrestled with the answer—to write a book on drugs, the culture, and the trauma that surrounds it—because I would rather enjoy writing about happier moments in life. But suddenly it dawned on me to take the evil that was used against my life and turn it around for good. Romans 8:28 reads: "And we know that all things work together for good to those who love God, to those who are the called according to His purpose." So it is with this purpose in mind that I humble myself and share things I dare not tell a soul, but here, I will tell you most of it.

You may be searching for answers, for solutions, or for how other people survive or live. You may have survived a traumatic relationship or other crimes of the heart. You may be dealing with children, family members, or friends who are on heroin or other substances. Or you may have been bullied from your youth or as a grown adult. Possibly, you have experienced being body-shamed for either becoming overweight or by being too thin. Maybe you have been raped, molested, or victimized by a bully or the so-called *mean* kids at school. Yet, out of all these distressing encounters know, there is beauty for ashes and joy for mourning, and the Lord can turn anyone's mourning into dancing once again!

Having been a Christian nearly my entire life, here is my journey of championing through life's opposition, obstacles, and conflicts that occurred within and without. Outside of drama unfolding, this is a book filled with God interventions, provisions, healing, and restoration. It takes prevailing faith, perseverance, and hope in the midst of difficult circumstances, heartbreak, and troubles to overcome. It is these characteristics that will stand the test of time. But, more importantly, it is because of God and His resurrection power to raise the dead that we can be set free. He breathed into my dead, lifeless, and dry bones and brought me out of the miry clay, giving me life and life abundantly. For this and much more, I am forever, eternally grateful. Above all, He will breathe new life into anyone who calls upon the name of the Lord!

In the end, at the end of the day, at the end of one's life, there is healing, there is health, and there is restoration. I know this is true because at one time I was a *prodigal*, and without a doubt, the Lord rescued and delivered me from the enemy.

May God bless you as you read this book!

ACKNOWLEDGEMENTS

To my husband, Danny: When we met, I pinched your arm and asked, "Are you for real?" And, come to find out, you are a *real* Christian. And then, in time, you asked me, "Would you have this *last* dance with me?" Well, of course, I said, "I do! Yes, I will have this last dance with you and more …"

From experience, I know this: God is a God of new beginnings, fresh starts, and do-overs. With that being said, I would like to honor my husband who gave me the freedom to enter the writer's world and supported me. All he ever heard was, "I'm working on a rough draft, a revision," or, "I'm removing a chapter and doing lots of editing." Especially when my income was at a stalemate, Dan was patient (to the best of my knowledge) with the ongoing, copious process of writing and has become my biggest fan.

Thank you for taking this journey with me.

I love you!

To the members of WestBow Press and to those who made my dream and this dialogue a reality: Thank you for your time, direction, and energy.

INTRODUCTION

Why cover bullies, abuse, and the addict? Today, the subject of bullying is relevant, and the definition has expanded over time to include abuse and addiction. The following chapters cover these topics *before* and *after* the creation of the internet and social media networks. This subject matter has not only affected me personally, but quite possibly, these subjects have touched you, your loved ones, or others you may know. Jesus Christ is the same yesterday, today, and tomorrow. And at the end of the day, He wants to restore us and make us whole.

Why did I write about drug abuse and heroin? My goal is to cast a spin on drugs and heroin as bullies and to expose the impact these bullies have had on others. Not only will you see that drugs can bully, but you will read what this bully does to the addict, the family, and those closest to the individual. Directly and indirectly, I have seen this bully up close. Drug abuse is a destructive force that can destroy a person or a family. I know. I have watched it torment and ruin others. Addictions are inside and outside the church, and it's time to talk about it. Outside of this, I know that God wants to heal and set people free.

What does the Bible say about bullying, abuse, or addiction? There are many scriptures pertaining to the above. Here are a few:

> Blessed are you when others revile you and persecute you and utter all kinds of evil against you falsely on my account. (Matt. 5:11 English Standard Version)

Be strong and of good courage, do not fear nor be afraid of them; for the Lord your God, He is the one who goes with you. He will not leave you nor forsake you. (Deut. 31:6)

If anyone stirs up strife, it is not from me; whoever stirs up strife with you shall fall because of you. Behold, I have created the smith who blows the fire of coals and produces a weapon for its purpose. I have also created the ravager to destroy; no weapon that is fashioned against you shall succeed, and you shall confute every tongue that rises against you in judgment. This is the heritage of the servants of the Lord and their vindication from me, declares the Lord. (Is. 54:15–17, ESV)

Woe to those who rise early in the morning, that they may follow intoxicating drink; who continue until night, till wine inflames them! (Is. 5:11)

And do not lead us not into temptation, but deliver us from the evil one. For yours is the kingdom and the power and the glory forever. Amen. (Matt. 6:13)

The thief does not come except to steal, and to kill, and to destroy. I have come that they may have life, and that they may have it more abundantly. (John 10:10)

What are some examples of bullying, sexual abuse, and addiction in the Bible? In 1 Samuel 17, David faces Goliath, a male bully. In 1 Kings 19, Elijah faces Jezebel, and again in 2 Kings 9, Jehu faces Jezebel, a female bully. In Luke 4, the mobs came against Jesus to throw Him over the cliff, yet He walked through the crowd and went His way. And, in Acts 7, the Sanhedrin, a group or mob, came against Stephan and stoned him to death. 2 Samuel 13:11–12, 14, 20, depicts Amnon sexually abusing Tamar. Also, in Genesis 34 is the story of the rape of Dinah. In the end, her perpetrator was held accountable and was killed. In Proverbs 23:29–35, you can read about the end result of habitual addiction.

What does the Bible say about restoration? There is a huge need for people to be restored on many levels, whether it is psychological, physical, or spiritual. In Christ, restoration is available for everyone. The Word is a light that brings truth, healing, and breakthrough. Healing leads to restoration of body, mind, and soul.

> For I will restore health to you, and your wounds I will heal, declares the Lord. (Jer. 30:17 ESV)

> I will restore to you the years that the swarming locust has eaten, the hopper, the destroyer, and the cutter, my great army, which I sent among you. You shall eat in plenty and be satisfied, and praise the name of the Lord your God, who has dealt wondrously with you. And my people shall never again be put to shame. (Joel 2:25–26 ESV)

Why did I allow bullying into my life? I didn't. Really, who asks for it? Do you think I had a target on my back? No! Was I looking to be bullied? No! So was it my size, the color of my skin or hair, my gender, my age, my success, or the fact that I was trying to live the Christian life? Well, none of the reasons that people use to harm others count as to be anyone's target. But the bully, with his or her sinful, flawed, sick, or evil sense of self, intentionally or unintentionally looks for a target to prey on. From youth and beyond, many times I was caught off guard and unprepared for the abnormal. Who really prepares beforehand to become *prey* for a bully? Every situation can be strikingly different, as you will read. Sometimes, you're stunned by the bully, or you can't believe this is happening to you as you are *broadsided* by the attack. Other times, you're not sure what to do in potentially volatile circumstances that you may wind up in. It's not a one-size-fits-all fix when confronted. The lack of rationality is lost in evil; it's not always predictable when witnessed in chaos.

Today, this is happening on a scale that is unprecedented, leaving moral corruption, lawlessness, and destruction in its path. To say, "I'm a survivor of bullying, of sexual abuse, and of addiction from my youth," is attributed to forgiving the injustice and offenders plus turning to the Lord for help, forgiveness, guidance, grace, and restoration. In the end, I became *proactive,* taking back the land that was stolen from my life.

What are some human aspects that impact those who have been bullied or abused? Bullying or abuse can take a toll on an individual, whether a child, a teenager, or an adult. It affects people both psychologically and physically, causing low self-esteem, depression, panic attacks, phobias, fear, and post-traumatic stress disorder, alongside other symptoms or ailments. The trauma of bullying and abuse can lead to physical impairments, addictions, suicidal ideation or attempts, or even suicide. All these aspects are either shared inside this book or documented in other outside resources. Beyond these dynamics, there is a God who desires to heal, restore, and set us free. Yes, the Lord wants to heal broken, hurting people and take away the pain. I've seen this not only in my life but in others, and I'm forever grateful to a God who truly loves, cares, and understands.

Definition of bullying and the characteristics of a bully or bullies: Bullying is one form of abuse. There are many faces a bully can wear. Bullying has a broad definition and is clearly defined in the United States and internationally. The definitions today are multifaceted and multicultural and cover all socioeconomic backgrounds. Bullying can be overt and also subtle, such as brainwashing, which is covert. It can be seen in aggressive violence and persecution, as well as in verbal criticism and disrespect.

Likewise, bullying masquerades itself and is clearly seen in physical and psychological (emotional and mental) abuse, misogyny, narcissism and narcissistic abuse, control and fear-based control, misuse of authority, manipulation, rejection, alienation, segregation, labeling (name-calling), slander, harassment, shame, and betrayal. It is clearly a form of projected hate. Sadly, bullying has led to countless deaths. And being bullied by drugs or heroin has led some to an early grave.

Bullying by the opponent is intentional or unintentional: This form of destructive behavior exhibited from a bully is intentional when it is deliberate, calculated, yet irrational and can become unpredictable when choosing to cause harm to another. It is unintentional if the abuser is ignorant, mentally challenged, uneducated, or in denial of his or her own negative, unwarranted, and unjustified conduct. The person sees the twisted actions as acceptable in his or her own eyes until taught otherwise. On a whole, acceptable behavior of what is right or wrong is losing definition by today's standards and biblical truths. Boundaries are becoming blurred as what's wrong becomes right as foretold in Isaiah 5:20.

Additionally, we need to protect ourselves and look out for the welfare of others. Education and appropriate boundaries will equip us to act and not react to the negative actions or influences of a bully or bullies, either privately or in the public sector.

Mobbing is a form of bullying: Outside of the physical acts of mobbing by a group of bullies, it also includes nonviolent tactics such as the spreading of rumors (lies), heckling, taunting, intimidation, manipulation, and verbal threats. Overall, these tactics are introduced by a ringleader(s) who initiates the mobbing of an individual.

Misogyny is a form of bullying: To a lesser or a greater degree, misogyny is seen as a form of bullying. It has permeated and intertwined itself like a web in the minds of men throughout the ages. And, absolutely, this does not apply to all men.

What is misogyny, you may ask? Misogyny is for a man to hate or dislike women. The meaning of this word is both archaic and barbaric in its heritage and use. Misogyny is considered outdated by some, yet it still exists. Misogynistic men will mistreat, mistrust, misuse, and berate females, deferring to being condescending and demeaning toward women. This includes control, verbal or physical abuse, and punishment. It is a stronghold of thought where women are inferior to men. Supporters of misogyny say, "Women are beneath men." They bully and abuse women on a variety of levels, from personal to work-related experiences. This has become a subculture of thoughts and actions that can still be seen universally today.

Drugs: Bullied by drugs? Yes, from pharmaceuticals to heroin and everything in-between. This bully is hard to deal with, and the consequences can be severe. If not dealt with, the outcome could be mortality. What if you had to face this bully in yourself or in another? How would you respond? When this bully grips your life, the user is changed, others around the user are changed, while the user (the addict) becomes haunted, controlled, shamed, and finally betrayed by the illusion illicit drugs portrays. These controlling substances bully the user psychologically and harness them physiologically through addictive cravings, which is covered in this book.

In this book are the many faces of a bully, abuse, and addiction: Although life may dictate some experiences outside of our control, it's never too late to turn life around or to turn ourselves around and become whole. No matter what has happened to us along the way, there is a way out. Here, I'm taking real-life situations, both past and present, that show the similarities and differences *before* and *after* the internet, yet they have the same outcome: broken and shattered lives. And I've been there. Although the severity and intensity of these subjects have escalated worldwide *after* the internet, the need for healing and restoration is available through Jesus Christ. He wants to heal us whether it was something that happened decades ago or just last week. The fact that I was restored by His power from traumatic events outside of my control is just one of the many reasons I took the journey to write this book.

Finally, we are all on separate journeys with a final destination in front of us—heaven. So let us run the race drawing grace from above, and may we let go of everything holding us down. Let's lay our burdens at the Lord's feet in order to run the race set before us to the finish line.

> Finally, brothers, rejoice. Aim for restoration, comfort one another, agree with one another, live in peace; and the God of love and peace will be with you.
> — 2 Corinthians 13:11 ESV

CHAPTER 1

BULLIED BY DRUGS: GRACE'S STORY

If you kneel before God, you can stand before anyone.
— TBN Networks

JESUS CAME TO SET US FREE!

"There are more people condemned to die in the prison of the heart and mind than in all the institutions combined together, *and I was one of them.*" This is how I opened at the mic inside a crowded auditorium. Here's my story of being bullied by drugs. I'm not proud of it, but I give all the glory to God for the outcome. Although I really wanted to ditch this chapter in the book and leave it out, I felt the Holy Spirit tugging on my heart not to leave it out. My prayer is this: May this testimony of healing and deliverance from drug abuse and the culture save a life or be used to help those who have never had to deal with an addict, but do so today.

Not all drug addicts have success stories, as you will read in some of the following chapters. However, contained in this testimony is a true success story!

A LITTLE BIT ABOUT ME

Our tiny family moved into a brand-new home in the mid-1960s. I grew up in the suburbs of a middle-class neighborhood. At that time, my sister and I attended a private Christian elementary school. I thank God for my Christian upbringing and for all the good things instilled inside me from my parents. Additionally, I thank Him that I was able to attend a Christian school during my younger years. Yet, on the flip side, you can read more about the educational system's ways and means to educate, which included bullying—sorry to say—in a chapter titled "My Informative Years." Those experiences took place *before* the internet was even invented. Yet, once upon a time, I was also called many not-so-nice fat-shaming names and more, and you can read about this in the chapter "Bullied for Being Fat and Rejected." Plus, you can compare this to "Fit, Thin, and Bullied," which took place *after* social media was established. And, remarkably, I was bullied for being thin. Imagine that.

When we were young, our family went to church three days a week, and if there was an itinerant preacher visiting, we were there for those additional nightly services too. Whenever the doors of the church were open, we were there. That played a huge part in my Christian heritage, as there were many groups I was involved with from my youth. A firm foundation was laid inside my heart at a tender age to *know* the Lord.

FAITH AND MIRACLES

I witnessed my first miracle at eight years old. That happened to me not once but twice, while growing up. I must add before you read that the following topic might sound a bit gross. Nonetheless, I sure received a miracle! Being young with a large visible wart on my leg, that imperfection was like looking at Mount Everest. I never wanted to wear shorts because of it and sought to hide my unsightly wart during the summer months. While lying in bed saying my nightly prayers, I prayed as I always did, "Dear heavenly Father." And then I asked, "Jesus, will you heal this ugly wart on my leg?" I told Him, "I *believe* You can heal me." Then I thanked Him for healing me like I was taught.

Much to my amazement, after I prayed, I reached over to inquisitively touch my leg. The ghastly wart was instantly gone—no sign or trace of it. My skin was smooth as silk. With that discovery, I bolted out of bed, threw open the door, and ran around the house screaming, "It's gone! It's gone! It's gone!"

"What's gone?" my parents asked.

"The wart is gone—completely gone," I shrieked and jumped with excitement.

My parents and sister rejoiced with me. I was exhilarated and overjoyed to be healed of something as small and insignificant as a wart.

Then later it happened a second time—unbelievably true! Only that time it was larger and uglier. The wart grew on my other leg for all eyes to see. And what's bigger than Mount Everest? That second wart. But I can't ignore the miracle. I was a bit older and unhappy to see one pop up again. I thought the imperfection was a shameful site to look at. To me, it stuck out like a sore thumb. So that time I tried a remedy—Compound W. It wasn't working at all, and I grew frustrated. Then one night while lying in bed saying my nightly prayers, I said, "Dear Lord Jesus, forgive me for not asking or trusting You to heal the wart on my leg. I should have asked you first instead of trusting in the Compound W." That is close to everything I prayed—no more. After my prayers were over, not thinking that Jesus would or could do it again, I reached over to feel my leg. And the wart was—again—completely gone. Once more, I jumped out of bed and ran around the house excited to hear my mother (who has since passed away) saying, "Thank you, Jesus." We all celebrated together in another instant miracle. Not a trace of the unsightly wart was left on my leg.

How could I ever forget those two instances of Jesus healing me as a child? I will always return to those two miracles from my youth. They gave me faith for bigger ones to come while growing up and as an adult. So don't despise the day of small beginnings. (See Zechariah 4:10.) You'll never know where that might lead you. Thank God for every experience both big and small. He's there for you and with you through everything you encounter. Today, I know my God, and I belong to Jesus, the author and finisher of my faith! This firm foundation in Christ, although it has been shaken, tested, and tried by fire, has kept me all these years.

ABANDONMENT AND SEPARATION

Little did I know, in our family dynamics a turn of events would take place that I had no control over. My mother and father were having problems. Those problems led to their separation. The separation was met with reconciliation, to be followed again by separation, concluding in divorce. This in and of itself is a powerful experience for any child, teen, or young adult. It definitely hit home with my older sister, Donna, and me. Remember the toy yo-yo? Before their divorce was final, my emotions would go up with each makeup session, and they would go down with each family separation, making me feel just like that toy yo-yo.

For years, in my head I was stuck inside their divorce. I couldn't escape it, I couldn't fix it, and I couldn't pretend it was a perfect world when it wasn't. Overall, divorce is a traumatic experience for anyone. That was certainly a defining moment, one I didn't want, and a life changing event to say the least. But it happened regardless. Life as I knew it would never be the same again.

First of all, you don't envision coming from a divorced home, but back in the day, it also carried a *huge* stigma. It still does, but not like it did years ago. Suddenly, our family dreams were gone. And the dreams my parents held for me were gone as well. All of that left me feeling abandoned and defective, like something was wrong. Our family became a minority statistic, as the percentage of Christians divorcing was quite small back then.

Because of that undiscussed stigma, I felt shame from others, embarrassed, judged, and humanly flawed, especially when I compared myself to other children coming from intact family homes. The Bible mentions to not compare ourselves to others, but I did. (See 2 Corinthians 10:12.) To me, others represented the perfect family unit— happy and unbroken. For years that haunted me, my imperfect self. Rarely did I hear of divorce in the sixties and seventies, and rarely did you hear of Christians in church divorcing. My tween years dissolved before my eyes as the family I was familiar with disintegrated and died.

Soon, I was a preadolescent and stealing my mother's cigarettes, so I could sneak into the backwoods to smoke with my friends behind our parents' backs. Smoking was taboo and highly frowned upon, especially for someone my age. Yet that one little secret (Mom's and mine) began before my parents' eminent divorce. The family dysfunction kept evolving behind the scenes too, just like my smoking. When my mother first started smoking and she found out I was smoking, she would hound me. And I would say, "You can't tell me not to smoke when you do!" The result was that our fighting over my smoking eventually came to an end. I was her determined, strong-willed child. Smoking stayed—and that was just for starters.

THE IMPACTFUL CHURCH EXPERIENCE

There was a short reprieve in my rebellion toward my parents' authority, as well as the private conflicts waging war inside our home—all before their great divorce was final. Alas, I was rebelling against my Christian upbringing. To top it off, during that time, my parents had forced me to attend a weekend getaway with our church youth group. Boarding a bus full of adolescents, I didn't even bother to wave goodbye. Why did they force me to go against my will? I was *so* mad at them for doing that to me and for wrecking my entire weekend. Come to find out, I wasn't the only one forced into going. My church friends were forced to go too. So I thought, *It can't be all that bad. We were all forced to go, and none of us looks happy. Did our parents cook this up together behind our backs?* Did their decision to make us go save us? Think about it. It saved me, but maybe not all of us. …

So, there I sat, suffocating on the dreaded bus ride crammed full of overly excited teens, when suddenly the youth pastor moved toward us and began pressuring our little rebel clique to know the Lord. He relentlessly pursued us the entire weekend. It seemed like wherever we went as a group, there he was, right behind us, coming again to talk to us. It was a wonderful idea, but I didn't see it like that back then. By the time the weekend was over, my friends appeared to be buckling under the pressure to conform to what the youth pastor was sharing. "All you have to do is invite Jesus in your heart and ask Him to forgive you of your sins. Ask Him in your heart to stay."

But I didn't want to listen, and I didn't want to participate. Except for on the way home, the bus was filled with the glory of the Lord. All of the kids on the bus were being filled with the Holy Spirit, just like you read in the Bible. When I saw my best girlfriend in the middle of the bus aisle go down on her knees and saw her countenance change right before my eyes, my first thought was, *Whatever happened to her, I want it too.* Visually, I could see the experience was real. And in my heart, I sensed, I knew, and I felt it was for real. I don't ever recall my knees hitting the floor of the bus, but there I was on my knees when all of a sudden, I knew I was immersed in the glory of the Lord! The presence of the Lord filled me too, as you can read in the second chapter of Acts in the Bible. We were all speaking in tongues on that anointed bus ride home. We were indeed changed. When we walked off the bus, we were completely and uniquely different. Our lives were radically transformed. We weren't the same as when we left, and it was self-evident. Beyond that, the pastor told our parents right away. Quite possibly, the pastor and our families were doing the happy dance that day. "Likewise, I say to you, there is joy in the presence of the angels of God over one sinner who repents" (Luke 15:10).

The youth pastor was a former heroin addict as well. Not only was he delivered out of his addiction and set free, but after that, he set out to change lives. My tiny world was changed because he didn't relent that weekend, and I finally listened. As you can read, God has a better plan and a better way for all of our lives.

Although the bus ride home was another unforgettable experience, I soon walked away from it all. The hard truth was that within a month's time, my friends and I who went on the bus trip backslid to our prior state—that of being a *prodigal.* We had a choice, and I forfeited my desire to be a true Christian because the bully—drugs—beckoned me. In retrospect, as I look back on that period of my life, we were never discipled on what to do after committing our lives to Christ. We needed some help getting started on the right track as young tweens and teens. Sure, I could recite scriptures and memory verses, but I didn't read the Word of God. I had it in my head but not fully in my heart. No one told us (or at least me) to read the Word and get the Word inside of us. Today, I know this is so vital. At that point, it was as if the good seed fell among the thorns. (See Matthew 13:1–23.) Then the heat came and scorched the seeds, and the seeds withered. Only here, I withered to a more rebellious state, just like the Bible proclaims in that parable. Yet here's a spoiler alert: it wasn't forever.

REACHING FOR THE GATEWAY DRUG

In seventh grade smoking cigarettes turned into smoking pot, which was just a stepping-stone into more. Add to that an occasional drink, and add to that experimenting with pills by eighth grade. The pills were what other kids brought to school from their parents' medicine cabinets. Some pills or narcotics sent students into ambulances and to the ER while in class. We would take them in the morning, sometimes a few and sometimes a handful, like a colorful cocktail of prescription drugs. They were all different shapes and sizes. I didn't seem to care, and (unbelievably) I didn't know what I was taking. I would receive the cocktail in the morning from just about any classmate who brought them in from home. Then, I would gulp them down at the water fountain and head off to class to see what was going to happen. My thoughts were, *Will I get off (catch a buzz) on these drugs or not?* I began to numb my pain to deal with the backlash of my parents' divorce drama and my personal secret trauma.

Never once did I consider the young gal, whom I once visited in a psych ward, who was left in a vegetative state by a drug overdose. She incoherently rattled at her words and made no sense. I tried to reach inside her head, her world, but I couldn't make a connection. It's a miracle I didn't end up like her then or later or in the future. I don't think she'll ever remember me if she's living because she couldn't recognize me at all. But I'll never forget her in looking back, and I will never forget the end result that drugs had upon her young life.

When our family finally broke up, all split up and shattered, I begrudgingly entered a new school for my freshman year. My sister, now a sophomore, stayed behind to live with my dad, and I moved away to live with my mother. By fifteen, I answered to nobody and became my own person, completely independent, delinquent, defiant, and insubordinate. I learned to play people. I played the game of telling adults what they needed to hear, or wanted to hear, and I did quite the opposite: lie, lie, lie.

THE BULLY—DRUGS—BULLIES

Today marijuana remains a communicative challenge for the Christian community. Medically, it's being embraced, and that's not the point of this book. The point of this chapter is that the Lord delivered me from drug abuse. Recreational weed is still illegal and only legal in some states, which means it's open for discussion. In the 1970s, it was illegal in every state—period. For me and for some, marijuana became a gateway drug to other substances. It was *unforeseeably* used as a gateway drug for me. Initially, I never saw beyond smoking pot. I never intended to become a full-fledged addict. Eventually, my hidden recreational habit led to speed or black beauties, the names often used for amphetamines, called uppers. These buzzwords are still in circulation today—no pun intended.

Soon, I began to mix speed with drinking and getting high. Some people call this polydrug abuse. Over time, I seemed to acquire a high tolerance for substances, which sent me on a search for stronger drugs. As time went on, more was better. Now I look back and think, *What did I do? What a waste of time. What a waste of life. I could have done better with the life given me.* It's never too late to change if you're doing drugs.

When I was with friends, we would party all night and not sleep at sleepovers. Rather, we laughed at our imaginary hallucinations throughout the night, which, quite honestly, is not a laughing matter in the end. Or I would plan to stay at my girlfriend's house, fully intending to do drugs all night, with her parents in another room, completely oblivious to our state of mind. For a long time, our parents never knew. My mother would think I was at a girlfriend's house or a football game or in school, and I was at some party instead. The boys were able to get their hands on stronger drugs to experiment with. In return, I used guys as friends, so I could use more potent strains of drugs that were in circulation. Drugs drove me to have the wrong kind of guys as friends.

If my mom only knew that was how I actually thought back in the day. Look at my high school memories. … Sad, aren't they? They are void of anything good—anything memorable.

So, there is cannabis, but there is also hash or hashish (which is stronger), Acapulco gold, and Thai stick, among other nicknames for reefer that were used then and now. As different potencies of pot became available, the high became higher after smoking it rolled in a joint, a pipe, or a bong. A bong is like vaping, only the apparatus used can be quite large, unlike an e-cigarette, which is as small as a USB drive.

Then there is angel dust. This substance, PCP (nicknamed angel dust), was made in the 1920s, brought to market in the 1950s, and discontinued in the 1960s. Originally it was used as an experimental anesthetic during surgery and was made up of almost a dozen different chemicals. The street dust contains *whatever* mind-altering, addictive compounds are laced into the marijuana, creating a psychedelic high. I say whatever because the user doesn't know what's actually being laced inside the weed or where it's from. What foreign country shipped the chemicals, friend or foe? You don't know. The addict doesn't know what is surging through his or her veins or being ingested inside the brain. I didn't know either. Did I care back then? No. Do others care? You would hope so, but most do not. Back then, I just cared about how high I was going to be, dust or no dust. Adding to this problem today, cannabis is now recreationally available in some states. Need I say more on this habit-forming recreational substance? Let it be read. It shouldn't be this readily available.

When I was in high school, it was nothing for me to get high by myself in the morning while getting ready for school after my mom left for work. Then after arriving to school in the morning, I'd get high again with the others. Later, I'd get high in-between classes because someone stole and kept the key to the girls' locked bathroom. On a side note, one day the admin must have decided to lock the girls' bathroom. Was it because of us? I'll never know, but we owned the key regardless after that. Yep, there was smokin' in the girls' room, not just "Smokin' in the Boys Room," as the song says.

Then at lunch I would be in a hurry. I'd nibble on someone's french fries or stuff a candy bar in my mouth, rushing to get outside in order to get high, followed by several more candy bars. The munchies led me to bum food in the cafeteria in order to save money for buying my next hit instead of food. After school, I met with friends to get high once more before we went home, and then, sometimes I'd get high before going to bed. That meant I was getting high all day. It also meant I was chasing the high just about every day for the next several years. I would secretly blow smoke out the window and chase it with a cigarette to cover up the odor. Nobody knew how deep I was in, and I didn't care—not yet.

Food wasn't the only thing I bummed. We used to bum car rides. In other words, we hitchhiked, and *we* were girls. At first, we traveled in pairs. Only later did I hitchhike by myself and without reservation, I'm sad to say. On one almost tragic day it was blistery hot, hotter than normal, and it was a long walk through town to my friend's house. We were going to hang out for the day. I just had to get there. Even though I wasn't hitchhiking that day, I did have some inner caution on accepting rides from strangers, but the heat was searing, and I threw caution to the wind.

"Never take a ride offered from a stranger," I was repeatedly told by my parents. But when I saw the large black dog sitting in the car, I thought, *This guy looks harmless; it can't be all that bad. The dog will be between us.* So I climbed in.

As the man headed toward my destination, the dog climbed on top of my lap. I gave it no real thought until the man began to pet the dog, and then he willfully and deliberately began grabbing me—the forbidden parts of me. Specifically, he crossed the line. All I remember is at that moment I went ballistic inside the car and began screaming. More so, I demanded that he pull over and let me out. It's a real *miracle* that he stopped the car and let me out. In hindsight, in my utter rebellion, disobedience, and defiance to my parents' words, the Lord protected me on that potentially catastrophic afternoon. I was a headstrong, stubborn prodigal, yet I was inwardly trembling and grateful to get out of a horrific, maybe deadly situation. That entire episode ended my hitchhiking career for good. And furthermore, it stopped me from taking any ride from any stranger forever. Now we have cell phones that track us, but back then, there was nothing like that. Without a doubt, I could have been raped, murdered, or both. If I did this today, I could be dead or almost dead by being sold into the sex trafficking world, held captive, or used and abused with my remains tossed into an unmarked grave in the middle of nowhere.

TRIPPING

To top it all off, I liked LSD. The street names for that drug include windowpane, acid, or blotter, as it was nicknamed in the seventies, and likewise today. The psychedelics were often in concert with other concoctions. I began to enter into full-blown hallucinogenic states with vivid, colorful, and lucid scenes. A few trips paralyzed me with fear, but I got off on the hallucinations that didn't exist. They were a nonreality, and yet they were my reality. Thankfully, those are not my memories today; they are the memories I escaped. It was escapism from my internal pain, but the real reality was my addiction covered my pain—a double whammy. I did try cocaine and quaaludes. Still, my preference was speed and LSD in combination with beer or cheap liquor and smoking weed. Admittedly, that sad underage scenario went on and on, so I've coined them *my wasted years*—seriously, no pun intended.

There is a God, and He rescued me, but I didn't want rescued then. I still hadn't had enough.

On one occasion, I was taking a driver's education class as a sophomore, when the instructor just appointed me next in line to drive a car full of students. Right then, I became their designated driver. I had placed a hit of LSD in my mouth right before I was informed, "You're up to drive." *Oops.* I didn't seem to care that I had just swallowed some windowpane. More so, what I did care about was hitting the peak of my drug trip while driving. It wasn't for the students' sake. What I really wanted was to enjoy my esoteric trip to a far-off place to nowhere and not be interrupted by anyone or anything. That was pretty selfish and uncaring of me. Was I deceived? No doubt.

See how you think when you're an addict? When you're high, you just don't care about anybody or the consequences of your actions. You don't think about the potential outcome of your behavior. You don't think that you might just wreck the car. You don't think that you could end up dead. You don't think about a car wreck killing another driver or killing those in the car with you. That's it. You don't think because you don't care. The drugs numb your senses and deaden your thoughts. You don't care that you or anyone else might end up as a statistic until it's too late. You think that type of thing will never happen to you, but it could if you're an addict.

I've seen it happen to others, and I still wasn't moved. It wasn't enough to cause me to stop, and that was inconceivably true.

Even the Bible says you can become uncaring, which certainly describes me at that point in my past. See, you don't care when you're high until maybe it's too late and you've lost everything. I'm saying this because I've been there, watching others ruin their lives, including me. Thankfully, when God gets hold of you, you are no longer the same as before. The old habits, the old ways of doing life, and the old you all become a new creation. Plus, the Lord will give you a new heart toward life, toward others, and toward Him. Yes, He will do a new thing in you if you ask Him and if you want it—just like He did in me a long time ago.

Another time, while trying to meet my high school friends at a nearby park to party, I dropped acid and began hallucinating that I was being chased by several policemen. In reality, I don't know if that was real or imaginary. So I ran all the way home because of a heightened fear of being chased by a group of male officers with batons. And with that intrusion of being chased by police, I lost a night with friends looking for a so-called good time.

Back in the day, there were no cell phones to reconnect with friends. If one of us became lost, was late, was a no-show, or got into trouble, the others just found out later. The end result was that there was only a *false* perception of having a good time while doing drugs. In other words, it's fake, it's phony, and it's deception. The bully drugs operates under the guise of lies and deceit. Drugs are cunningly able to rob, kill, and destroy a life, just like it says in John 10:10: "The thief does not come except to steal, and to kill, and to destroy. I have come that they may have life, and that they may have it more abundantly."

Another time while tripping on acid, a group of us were trying to jump a fence in order to enter a concert without paying. None of us had any money because we'd spent it all on drugs before we decided to sneak in. Soon, we were being chased by guards blowing their whistles at us and their dogs barking fiercely at us in the thick of the woods. Instead of jumping the fence, we ran for our lives. Here again, I'm not sure if that was real or imaginary, but nobody jumped the fence that night and entered the concert. Instead, we all ran out of the woods as fast as we could.

At the time, I wondered, *Were we being chased after all? Did we really just live through that, or am I hallucinating?* What was real, and what was not? I couldn't tell. And now I think, I could have done better with my life. I wish I had made better choices and stayed away from drugs.

What I didn't know was that alongside the LSD intoxication there would later come recurring hallucinogenic flashbacks. What is a flashback? It is a vivid replay of a psychedelic occurrence after a trip that happens days or weeks after ingesting acid. Not a ton, but the visual phenomenon did fade out of sight after I stopped using and became a Christian. Look at my regrettable memories of my wasted years. Basically, I'm saying, "Don't do what I did if I can reason with you. The road I traveled leads down a dead-end street. Choose a better path in life, so you have no regrets on your journey!"

When I was in high school, my mother abruptly told me, "You'll never amount to anything." In looking back, my mom may have said that out of sheer exasperation because I played around with drugs, *and* she finally found out and was livid. However, I disagree with her sentence. It wounded me. Back then, she couldn't control me, but she could control my driver's license. And that is exactly what happened, which made me one furious teenager. However, her actions didn't stop my reaction. I drove someone else's car later that night with just a driver's permit, not a valid license. Yet, on the day she confronted me, she also informed me, "If you leave and go to that concert, I will not sign for your license for an entire year." Her threat didn't stop my attending a Rolling Stones concert—no way, no how. Being defiant, I left with the group for the concert anyway.

Of course, the driver was already stoned when he came to pick us up, and I didn't even know the driver or some of the people in the car when they arrived. They were from a completely different school, or maybe they weren't even in school. They never said. My mom would have wanted to know their ages, where they lived, or if they went to school. Yet we'll never know. I do know my mom said, "You can't go or else ..."

Anyhow, my friends and I plummeted into the tiny beater car and began passing a joint around as we headed down the road. As the evening progressed, so did some heavy drugs. The guys had drugs they didn't care to share with all of us, and they were in an impaired, cognitive stupor by the end of the concert. They had mentally checked out. As a result, I was the only one sober enough to see the road to drive, and drive I did (without a license).

While everyone else sat motionless, passed out in the back seat of the car while lying on top of each other, I was the only one alert and coherent enough to see the road. However, the road wasn't clear enough for me to see due to the weather. One guy, the owner of the car, was going to drive, but I intercepted because he was too inebriated to see or to walk. I had no idea what they were stoned on. Later, I was glad they passed me over when sharing their secret stash of whatever it was. In retrospect, they spared me a possible overdose or even death.

At the time, I remember thinking, *Look at them. I believe I'm the only one capable of getting us home in one piece. They're too wasted. I'm wasted, but I know I can drive.* I could've been wrong—way wrong. I never stopped to think: *What if we crash? What if I really can't drive? What if we are pulled over? What if I end up in jail? What if I kill someone?* The road was a blur at times that night, so what if. …

There were others I know who did not make it home—stoners who were too intoxicated and were decapitated as their car smashed head-on into a brick wall. Still others I know were too drunk to drive as they drove their classmates over a cliff and ended up DOA. We all cried with such horrific news reports, and with that, the entire school would close its doors to mourn their loss.

Now, back to the words etched inside my mind from my mom: "You'll never amount to anything." That *song,* those words, became stuck in my head. That lingering statement didn't help. The words hurt, but the words didn't stop me. I continued to do drugs. Why? The drugs numbed my internal conflicts. That way, I couldn't feel anything. I dare not *feel* a thing. I'd rather dull the emotional pain of dead words (not words of life) resounding inside my head. Getting high was *not* the remedy to my problems. It was a *fake* (deceptive) solution. Jesus was the answer, but I wasn't open. I didn't listen. I shut Him out of my heart and tuned Him out. I didn't know or believe that Jesus could take away the pain of the past. And that new *song,* I wouldn't sing until the future.

In looking back, I'm grateful that's all I experienced as a bad trip. I'm saying this because some people never have a brain left while doing drugs. Drugs can lead to brain damage and death. Unfortunately, I have seen both up close. I give all the honor and glory to God today that I have my mind. He restored and delivered me. Your mind is a precious gift. Health is a gift. My advice is this: Don't take for granted the gifts God has given you. They are beautiful, wonderful, and irreplaceable!

WHITE SNIFF

For a season, as a suburban addict, I considered selling drugs for a little extra cash. My friend and I acquired some cocaine. As we snorted a line of coke before we cut it, we also kept some back and replaced it with another white substance. We must have used baking soda, baking powder, or corn starch, I'm not sure which, but it worked. It looked harmless, yet it looked the same; nonetheless, it was still harmful. That technique was not learned on the internet. There was no YouTube. Had the coke already been cut by others? I wouldn't have known. If so, what did they lace it with? Actually, did I have a pure substance to begin with, or did I have poison? What if it was poison? You don't think like that at the time, you just want the drug to take effect. Afterward, we flipped the packages of freshly cut cocaine. But I was dreading that move and somewhat panic-stricken about being found out. Of course, I wouldn't tell anyone, but could I trust my partner in crime? We weren't close, and I barely knew the individual. Meaning, I wasn't entirely sure about our arrangement.

I thought to myself, *We have changed the value of this compound and could possibly be in dire trouble, either criminally or by association.* That fact led to my decision that selling cocaine was not for me. I'm glad I didn't pursue that course of action to obtain illegal money for drugs. I'm also glad I didn't kill anyone with what I sold because others may have tampered with it too. In this day and age, the additives can kill you. But being young and on drugs, you only think about your next high. How are you going to get it? Who are you going to get it from, and where are you going to get the money to pay for your habit? These are some of the thoughts that can consume an addict. Look at my wasted years—realistically, no pun intended.

TEEN CHALLENGE

Innately and unbelievably, I knew to say no to heroin. That notion was engraved inside my head from a book David Wilkerson had published about his ministry, Teen Challenge. His ideal ministry was to take the Gospel on the streets and reach out to drug-addicted teens and gang members. David Wilkerson launched Teen Challenge in New York in 1960, and they are still viably helping addicts find freedom today in the United States, as well as in 110 other countries. My parents had given me his book when I was in elementary school. As I looked through the pages embattled with unsightly snapshots of emaciated, toothless people, I saw they were bald and hairless, frail and lifeless, and they looked morbid from shooting up heroin. Covered with scars, scabs, and track marks, their faces and their bodies scared me to sobriety when offered it. It embodied everything you would *never* want to become. So with that being said, I did everything but heroin. Go figure.

However, the pictures left an indelible, impressionable imprint upon my young mind, one which I could not erase from my person. Everyone should see pictures showing the end stages of a life ravaged by drugs. Pictures like the ones I'm mentioning may save a life if given the opportunity to try heroin or meth or whatever. Especially if someone becomes either vulnerable or curious about its effects, that person may reflect back to those lifeless photos. I know I did! A picture can paint a thousand inexpressible words. Without a doubt, I owe Teen Challenge a thank-you for printing and publishing such a book. I believe the vivid, detailed photographs stopped me from doing heroin. When I was faced with the opportunity to shoot up for free in high school, I passed (remembering the pictures), realizing the end result could cause an early, untimely death—mine. You know, that's how you get hooked—it's by trying one free shot. That's how you become a slave to heroin, and heroin is a real bully to contend with.

THE MANY FACES OF PAIN

In spite of a book loaded with graphic pictures and warnings, nothing prevented me from doing other drugs. I just planned to stay away from heroin. In seventh grade those around me were smoking pot, and that's when I gave it a try. Soon, it became a daily occurrence and a way to escape traumatic life events. That way, I couldn't feel the pain of my parents' divorce, its aftermath, and its dysfunction, which led to the collapse of our family unit, leaving us frayed, separated, and detached from one another. I couldn't feel the emotional pain of the molestation from a criminal pedophile, as it remained buried in my childhood, still unspoken, yet written within the pages of this book. I couldn't feel the physical and psychological pain of the rape I experienced in high school. I couldn't feel the sting, taunts, and hatred of being bullied by a group of vicious, *mean* girls. I couldn't feel the threat from the others who came to my house wielding a knife meant for me, all for saying hi to a guy friend from junior high.

Because I couldn't feel the intense emotional pain of their abuse, I reasoned, "Being stoned was better than being sober," numbing my pain and loathing reality. Who could I tell? No one spoke openly about those subjects back then, unlike today. There were way too many uncomfortable situations, emotions, and conflicts raging within and around me. There were many feelings I wanted to burry inside, pretending they didn't have a face or a name.

Instead of having tools available to address my pain, such as counseling, books, a support system, and the Lord, I turned to drugs. That was and is the *wrong* solution for pain that's not dealt with. The tools weren't available or accessible, and I blocked out the Lord. Rather, I convinced myself to ignore and suppress the trauma. Society added to it and said, "You're not supposed to talk about it." That didn't help, as you can read, or you may know for yourself. To add to the silence, I was also told, "Don't talk about it." So to deaden the pain and escape reality, I desensitized my thoughts in order to not feel a thing and silenced my memories.

To escape is to avoid the inevitable. The painful wounds still needed addressed when I was sober. They didn't go away. They didn't just disappear. In time, they became hard to ignore, and I couldn't wish the wounds away. They remained hidden, lingering, and buried inside my soul. What's even more deceptive? I liked the mind-altering state of being high. In the end, I hated life, hated me, and hated what I'd become. Where was real agape love? Who could take away the pain? Only Jesus could! Only, I didn't look to Him. I also didn't know He could help me. I didn't know that He would take away years of pain and that He actually wanted to help me overcome. Instead, I ignored Him. I still hadn't had enough.

Today, online and in the news, there are people questioning what makes an addict (because the person is curious or trying to understand) and what contributes to addiction. Well, here, I share the making of an addict and the reasons why I used. Yet, in spite of it all, Jesus had a better plan for my life, and in time, the best was yet to come. The better plan was His, not mine, but I refused to see it.

Over time, my attitude became, "I don't care." I seemed to adopt that attitude and apply it to almost everything. It's true that when you're involved with drugs, you lie, steal, and cheat to maintain your lifestyle. I lied to get in and out of situations. I stole money to buy drugs, and I stole things to show for the money that I was given, if given anything. I sat by the A students intentionally if I needed their test scores. My reasoning was that I wanted to maintain decent enough grades to pass to the next grade because I missed the maximum number of days allowed, and I didn't care. To pull that off, I began calling in like a parent, excusing myself from school, and then writing my own notes as to why I was absent. The absence was always due to some nonexistent, lame ailment that never truly existed. The rebel in me turned into more of a manipulator, liar, and a thief, just so I could get away with everything that I wanted to do, and I didn't care. My goal was to not get caught, and that I sort of cared about.

Seriously, I didn't care about too much outside of getting high, staying high, and doing my own thing. I did think about dropping out of school but concluded that would not work in my favor in the long run. At least I thought that one through. And, honestly, I'm thankful I didn't quit school because back in the day, you couldn't even get a job or go to college without physical proof of your diploma in hand. Besides, I eventually went off to college.

SOME GOOD, SOME NOT

In junior high I had one teacher I liked, and everybody came to his class. He was extremely comical, and nobody skipped his class, including me. I know he is no longer living, but he was behind my inspiration and passion to write. That is where it all began. My formidable desire to write truly started inside his classroom. Plus, his classes were never boring. He never put me to sleep like some teachers could—just saying. He was funny, he made learning an adventure, and he was socially relatable.

In the beginning, he related to some in the wrong way (an illegal way), but it was in an awesome way in the end. At first, I began to date and hang around some of the college students I met at his parties. Present were drugs and alcohol, and to top that off, I was still underage and wasn't supposed to be there, or so I was told. It was all part of an off-campus secret society of partiers. Eventually, my attendance was somewhat frowned upon, but I snuck in anyway to party and got away with it. If I saw my teacher begin to enter a room, I generally ducked or turned my back to avoid being seen by him. Needless to say, he was well liked as our teacher inside and outside of school.

Still, in my rebellious thinking (my old self), I set out to fix the underage dilemma for the future. I maneuvered that by tracking down my own fake ID with the help of some people I didn't even know. I blindly put myself at risk by working with strangers, which was not a good choice at all. Yet the fake ID enabled me to enter the bar scene, to attend my teacher's parties (or so I thought), and to buy alcohol. What I didn't know and what never entered my head was the possibility of going to prison for its possession and usage or paying a huge fine. I was young and naïve at sixteen when I flashed my newly fashioned fake ID, which my mother never did hear about or see. I am sure she would not have been happy about that arrangement either, made in my insubordination, and she probably would have grounded me for what may have felt like forever if she ever found out. However, to put myself in jeopardy, all it took was a little bit of makeup and some inner courage, and voila, I was in big trouble if I got caught.

Remarkably, something wonderful and good came out of knowing that teacher. In the future, he became a Christian and a pastor. His life was radically transformed. In return, he set out to touch lives with the truth, and what a great ending to his story.

On the other hand, in junior high there was one teacher I didn't like, except he taught one of the subjects I loved: art. Although I loved my art classes, the teacher was a real bad apple to the core, void of morals and principles and integrity. And that was because he preyed on me, a teenager, by intentionally asking me into the storage room where he attempted to proposition me for sex. Since that time, he has passed away, but those days of being pursued by that teacher was just another reason why I numbed my shock over his behavior and self-medicated with an ongoing addiction. I didn't want to feel.

The discouragement I carried within me as a teen was a result of having my senses emotionally violated and not being able to talk about it to anyone. There were no hotlines to call, and never once did I hear of any teen sharing about wrongful interactions such as the one I was stuck in. There was no safe place in school to turn to for assistance and no internet highway of information to pursue back then, or I would have quickly searched online for that information. Now we have the availability of crisis intervention hotlines on the web, which are directed toward every county, city, state, or local church. Regardless, I tried my best to shrug it off and ignore a growing dilemma.

At first, I couldn't quite put my finger on what he was up to because I was so naive. Initially, he started off with subtle statements such as, "You look very nice today," followed by bolder inquiries like, "What are you doing after school?" Later, it was flat out, "Would you like to ride around with us and get high after school?" That meant two male teachers with me, driving around after school together. That didn't sound safe; it sounded horrible to my ringing ears in the end. The second teacher I never did meet, which spared me more drama. Then finally, the teacher took his conversation to another level when he said, "Let's go out and get high together and …" Which clearly escalated to his improper agenda with me (a minor): drugs in exchange for sex.

When those words fell out of his mouth, I was totally caught off guard. Now, that is twisted, perverted, and repulsive—not normal. That was not normal behavior for a male professional. In growing up, I was taught to trust teachers, so after that, I was more than overwhelmed. When the art teacher invited me to go out and party, I always declined and walked away as fast as I could. Dealing with him sent shivers down my spine. Even though the drugs would have been free (from a teacher, sad to say), his actions toward me became downright despicable and wrong and, furthermore, illegal. He turned into a super creepy person, making me feel unsafe and uneasy. And there were times I felt entirely unsure of what to do with what he was saying inside of school. That particular teacher was at least thirty to thirty-five years my senior at the time of his indecent proposal. I would have never conceded no matter what. What's more, even if he were handsome and built like steel, I still would not have conceded no matter what with a grown-up.

Perhaps those were my innate boundaries? Thank God I paid attention to those gut feelings. I grimaced and shrugged off every intrusive attempt that the teacher made while going inside the storage room for art supplies. When his huge, disturbing presence blocked the doorway so I couldn't leave when I wanted to (which happened more than once), I would panic inside while waiting to escape his confrontations. Upon getting out of that stuffy little room, I would quickly run back into the art class full of students, pretending everything was okay. I acted calm, cool, and collected when I was anything but that. After high school, that sorry saga remained buried inside me for years to come. Back then, I avoided that particular teacher at all costs, but not the art I loved creating.

Although those events were awkward and emotionally traumatizing, they were hard to forget. I couldn't forget. However, the memory would one day be healed of that teacher trying to coerce and manipulate me, a student, into an illicit situation when, truthfully, all I really wanted to do was innocently paint with expression and color. There were no guidelines or forums back in the day on stranger danger. Such programs have since been created to protect students from teachers who sexually proposition or harass a student. Back then, I wouldn't have been listened to; it's more likely I would have been penalized. It would have all come back in my face to shut me down. In the end, I ignored the harassment, knowing the teacher would somehow get away with what he had done even if I did tell someone. Whether it boiled down to his status or tenure or money, or all of that protecting him, I will never know. Regardless, I learned to avoid his advances and dodged being asked into the backroom for whatever reason.

I didn't say all of the above to be in my head. It was that God got it out of my head in the end. In addition, I was able to forgive the teacher for his unjust actions. And last of all on this subject, even though that circumstance was difficult to revise and write down, when I did say yes to knowing and living for Christ, more was to come. He took away the emotional burden and the memory that I was carrying around in my head after I came to Him in prayer. This I know: the Lord will take anyone's burden away for good.

BURNOUT

It wouldn't be fitting to elaborate on everything I did or experienced while doing drugs in high school. Still, you can read about other experiences in the chapters titled "The Mean Girls in School (Mob Bullying)" and "Unbelievably, They Came with a Knife." Both chapters are about mob (or group) bullying in school. If you add these chapters to other life events, alongside the bully drugs, the entire combination took me into a dark, downward spiral. As time passed, drugs were getting the best of me. So by the time I reached eleventh grade, I was pretty much known as the class burnout.

I'm not proud of disclosing or sharing any of these details, but I am. Why did classmates call me a burnout? At first, I didn't understand why they pinned that label on me. Why me? They weren't talking about emotional or physical burnout (and maybe some of that was true), but an addict burned out and exhausted from habitual drug abuse. Furthermore, when I found out they were talking about me (that other kids saw me as a real burnout), I was in complete denial of their insinuations. Most of the people I hung around with were good at making up stories, making up false accusations, or simply not telling the truth—in other words, lying to your face. And yet, were they lying to me at that moment? How could I believe them? It became hard to tell their truths from lies. These were addicts speaking to me, and addicts lie. They lie to hide their secrets, they lie to obtain money, and they lie as to their whereabouts. How do I know? I've been there. It's part of the culture of addiction, both then and now.

Anyhow, their words became a blur for me to decipher, more of a smokescreen to interpret, or was that now my reality? It couldn't be me. It couldn't be true, but it was. Yes, it was difficult to admit that I despised myself for turning into a total, wasted burnout. What had become of my life? It was a struggle to realize that I turned into a mess.

It was even harder to hear it from my peers who were still binging on drugs themselves yet putting me down for doing them as well. "You're too burnt out to hang with us," they told me. "We don't want to be your friend if you continue to stay wasted all the time."

It was nothing to get stoned in school like I had said earlier, sitting blank-faced and starring out a window. That is what became of me with my continued drug use. That is when you know you're at your absolute worst—when you truly become a zombie and you portray that zombielike stare. I actually did have that zombielike stare. That *look,* that pale, ashen look overcame me.

Then one day, a group of us were getting stoned in someone's car, which was parked inside the school parking lot during lunchtime. It's a wonder we didn't get in trouble for our blatant using on school grounds. But it was in the car, in the midst of a cloud of vaporous smoke, that I sat stone-faced, thinking, *I don't like the person I've become. I don't like me. I don't like me like this any longer. I'm so burned out that I don't even talk. I just sit and stare like I'm dead. I feel mostly dead. This can't be it in life. There's got to be more to life than sitting here wasted.* Life was spiraling out of control, and I could certainly see it for real that time as I just sat there smelling like a dead zombie in despair. *And* it was right there in the utter darkness that I suddenly had my life changing aha moment.

> If I ascend into heaven, You are there; if I make my bed in hell, behold, You are there.
>
> — Psalms 139:8

BEYOND THE PRESENT DARKNESS

While in the car trashed, I visualized that I was falling through a dark tunnel with no end in sight, inwardly knowing that the dark tunnel was death by drugs. All I could see was darkness surrounding me, engulfing me, but up above I could see light shining in the midst of total darkness. There was light piercing through darkness, and that *light* pierced my heart. Was that the glory of the Lord piercing my dark world? I *knew* it had to be the Lord! He was calling me out of my darkness, my Sheol. (See Jonah

2:2–6.) That's when it happened … and that time I paid attention. That time I said yes. Right there inside the smoldering car I felt the Holy Spirit nudging me, drawing me, and calling me out of the grave I'd climbed into and into His marvelous light. So I ran out of that grave! The prodigal emerged transformed, as in the parable of the lost son (or daughter), and I answered His call. (See Luke 15:11–32.)

> But you are a chosen generation, a royal priesthood, a holy nation, His own special people, that you may proclaim the praises of Him who called you out of darkness into His marvelous light. (1 Peter 2:9)

Upon entering school the following day, something in the atmosphere had shifted. It was as if I had a muzzle over my ears, and it was hard to hear anything that day. The only thing I heard was the name of Jesus over and over again. Something spectacular was taking place that day. Both in the halls and in the classroom, when people were talking, I either heard people taking the Lord's name in vain or heard people saying the name of Jesus and praising His name. His presence was tangible. I felt His presence in the school! It was almost like a daydream, yet all I could hear was His name: Jesus. He was pursuing me. Something was changing, and that something was someone like me—just like in the parable of the lost sheep. (See Luke 15:1–7.) He went inside that car and in that school and found me. Jesus cared enough to go inside my world to rescue me out of my mess. *And, above all, that time I was listening and choosing to follow Him out of the grave.*

The only thing I knew to do was return to my old church, the one where I was forced to attend a youth camp by my parents. It turned out that weekend wasn't a total waste. God got a hold of me on the bus ride home. It was a ride I will never forget because God is *not* dead. His presence showed up on the bus. I know it was the Holy Spirit back then, leading me at that moment and guiding me to return to church. The desire to attend church and go back to that youth group burned within me.

As soon as possible, I made the long drive and attended a midweek service. By that time, I was given permission to drive. When I arrived, everyone was singing. As I sat in the pew, I couldn't sing. I tried opening my mouth, yet nothing came out. Tears began streaming down my face as I sat in silence. During the middle of the song, I stood up and walked right up front to my former youth pastor, the same one who had gone on the bus trip years ago and had been delivered from heroin. I said to him, "I can't sing. I'm not sure why I can't sing. I'm here, but I don't know what to do next. I can't get the words out of my mouth." It was during the singing that I welcomed Jesus back in my heart to stay and repented of my sins. Remarkably, everything changed.

EVERYTHING WAS CHANGING

When I returned to school the following day, my heart was singing. I had changed for the better. I no longer needed or wanted drugs, alcohol, or even cigarettes (and I used to chain-smoke a pack or more a day). My consuming desire for all of those substances was completely gone. I was delivered from my addictions, and I did not go through any type of withdrawal symptoms whatsoever. Imagine that! To me, it was a miracle. That instantaneous deliverance was in and of itself a demonstration of Christ's resurrection power and amazing grace. Grace is unmerited favor, meaning I didn't deserve any of it.

After that, I began to show up to class on time, and I actually went to all of my classes for the first time in years. No more skipping classes or days when I wanted to. Back in the day, we called it flicking classes or flicking school. Never again did I have to deal with detentions and suspensions like during my rebellion. Gone were the days of lying to cover for my truant behavior. Those fantastic changes caused me to smile once more. It wasn't fake or phony or plastic, and that time my smile radiated from within. I no longer needed to lie, cheat, or steal or to be beaten down by the bully drugs. It was for real back then and still is to this day.

There was something else I noticed: there was no fear in sharing Jesus with anyone who would listen, either inside or outside of school. And due to that fearlessness, a chain reaction developed, like a domino effect. My favorite teacher, whom I told you about, went on to become a pastor. Many of the peers I hung around with, both in high school and college, became Christians due to watching the transformation God had worked inside of me. My countenance changed, and I no longer looked like a deadbeat zombie. I sounded different too due to the fact I cleaned up my mouth. What I said was no longer foulmouthed and full of four-letter words—in other words, profanity. I was no longer the burnout people labeled me as. Instead, I was a person with a voice telling others about Jesus and what He could do in *them*.

Because of those awesome changes, a dozen people made a choice to ask Jesus in their hearts. In return, they went on to touch others with the Gospel, and Christ was magnified. A few were the students who had bullied me in the past—the mean girls. Who would have known, and how could I have guessed, that something good would come out of something horrible?

That chain reaction continued to blossom, as we were part of the Jesus movement that was impacting the United States and other countries, but I wouldn't have known that back then. Thereafter, I found a new church that was on fire for the Lord and brought my friends. That anointed church opened a coffeehouse and introduced us to a culture of Christian rock music, which was foreign to our ears but had sprung from the movement. Finding that church was a lifesaver because they greatly helped all of us who left the drug scene behind, as we were entrenched in the rock and roll music of the seventies. I'm grateful for the many Christian pioneers in the music industry. Why? Because they helped pave the way for generations, both then and now, by giving everyone something to listen to outside of what the drug culture boasts about, namely sex, drugs, and rock and roll.

When my life changed, I also changed what I put in my head. No more garbage in (my head) or garbage out (my mouth). Over time, I changed my friends who were pulling me down; I changed where I went and who I hung around with. I got rid of my paraphernalia and anything that pertained to my past lifestyle of drugs. In other words, I cleaned house. I changed what I read, what I watched, and what I belonged too. Suddenly, I had a voracious appetite to read the Bible. In the past, I did not read the Bible, and that changed as I had a new desire to immerse myself in the Word. Psalms 119:11 says: "Your word I have hidden in my heart that I might not sin against You." The Word brought healing and guidance, therefore transforming me. There is life in the Word. God loved me right where I was at, *unconditionally*, mess and all. And little by little, I learned a new way to do life.

> Create in me a clean heart, O God, and renew a steadfast
> spirit within me. (Ps. 51:10)

There was such a turnaround in my overall persona and abilities that school became successful once more. Academically, I was achieving As and Bs without cheating, and with my credits, I positioned myself to graduate early. This also meant going to summer school, but I was ready to move forward and bear the heat of the classes without air-conditioning to get it done. Yet it was here, in the midst of many great things happening, that something tragic took place when I momentarily messed up and relapsed. Who could have thought that after all the good, after all of the changes, and after making a total commitment to Christ, that I would succumb to drugs once more and relapse? But I did just that—I relapsed. Outside of a very few people (the ones I did the drugs with), nobody really knew that I messed up and relapsed. It was to them and to God that I felt I ruined my entire testimony for good.

So, while many wonderful things were taking place in my life, it was here that I briefly sabotaged things. It was a moment in time, but I own it with the exception of the tragic part, which was completely out of my control and I didn't see coming, *and* that part ruined me for a while. The tragedy took place while in summer school to finish my course load and graduate early. That was when I backslid temporarily for a few months, and I wish I would not have done what I did. In other words, I screwed up and returned to some of my old ways—my old self. Hence, it was the backslidden relapse of a prodigal. As a baby Christian with Christian friends, the ones I had witnessed to alongside some of my *old* friends (the ones we all used to party with), it was that scenario that enticed a few of us to stumble. Regrettably, we began to get high together again. As new believers, we weren't ready to hang out with our friends from the past—those who could potentially bring us down by tempting us with our former addictions to drugs and alcohol. We needed a clean break, and I needed a fresh start. I needed to stay away from all temptation and move forward in life, not backward.

> No temptation has overtaken you except such as is
> common to man; but God is faithful, who will not allow

you to be tempted beyond what you are able, but with the temptation will also make the way of escape that you may be able to bear it. (1 Cor. 10:13)

In the beginning, I was strong and separated myself from certain individuals, but in my weakness, I fell for it. To me, it was sort of like a setup from the devil seeking who he could devour and destroy. Yet on one ominous night, a few of us were getting loaded, and toward curfew I was in dire jeopardy. Everyone went home except for me. I didn't see it to be a problem until it was too late. I stayed behind and was raped. I had no control over my circumstances when that happened, as you will read later on. And in a few days, I ended up in the ER. But I opened up about that night in the chapter titled "Bullied in the Basement: Rape and Drugs in Senior High." It's one of the many dangers of opening oneself up to drugs and the culture that comes with it. So with that being said, buyers beware. You just hope to live to tell about it.

After a night of binging and after the rape, I drove myself to summer school the next day and told no one. Sitting in a hot classroom on a muggy summer day, the room began to swirl, and I was about to get sick. Staggering out of the room, I ran outside behind the building, crouched down, and hunched over to vomit into the dirt between the bushes. Loudly, as if audibly, I heard these words: "As the dog returns to its vomit … Are *you*?" This verse can be found in 2 Peter 2:22 and also in Proverbs 26:11. Those words echoing throughout my head grabbed my attention. It was as if the Lord was saying to me, "Are you going to return to everything you just came out of—the drugs, the alcohol, that lifestyle? Everything you walked away from and left behind? Haven't you had enough? Don't go back to what I delivered you out of and set you free from."

Well, those thoughts, those words, and that moment definitely startled me and stopped me in my tracks. I felt that surely I had failed—failed God, failed me, and failed others watching me stumble as a new Christian. When I thought I had ruined my testimony, I discovered His grace was sufficient for me in my weakness, especially after I tripped up and made mistakes. Besides, I never wanted to ruin my testimony and all that God was doing in my life because I knew it was for real. The nearly audible

Word sobered me so much that I never returned back to the bully, drugs. Once and for all, it was over for me—for good.

In the future after graduation, it appeared that everyone was making plans and moving on with their lives. Absolutely, it was time for me to do the same. So I started looking for a Christian college to attend in another state. That decision brought a fresh start and a new journey to experience far away from home. Although it meant I would be moving away from what was familiar, I was ready to embrace those challenges and excited for the changes to come. It was the dawning of a new year.

RESTORATION

God can take what Satan meant for evil (such as trying to destroy my life) and turn it around for good. After college, I took those *lost years,* which I deemed my wasted years, and in return worked with youth paying it forward. In time, another door opened for me to travel with a Christian theatrical group. We performed in front of countless teens and college students, covering troublesome topics and spreading the truth through the creative arts.

In sharing, I opened at the mic with these words: "There are far more people condemned and dying in the prison of the heart and mind than in all the institutions put together, *and I was one of them."* This is my testimony of what I walked away from and left behind and how I was delivered, set free, and healed from traumatic events. Yet I also reached out to the audience, saying, "Learn from my story, and please stay away from (the bully) drugs. They will rob, steal, and destroy you, maybe even kill you. Instead, look up to Jesus who can change and deliver you, thereby giving you *freedom* and a future. He can take away your pain! He can break the power of addiction. No matter how broken or messed up life becomes, it's never too late. There *is* a God who restores life! But the fact remains that it's a choice to ask Jesus in your heart and to follow after Him."

> Therefore we also, since we are surrounded by so great
> a cloud of witnesses, let us lay aside every weight, and
> the sin which so easily ensnares us, and let us run with

endurance the race that is set before us, looking unto Jesus, the author and finisher of our faith, who for the joy that was set before Him endured the cross, despising the shame, and has sat down at the right hand of the throne of God. (Heb. 12:1–2)

IN CONCLUSION

When looking back, I chose to forgive. I didn't want to carry whatever happened to me around in my head or heart for all time. I didn't want an offense or traumatic circumstance to define or hold me back in life. The goal was to forgive and let go of the past. What evolved out of those experiences turned into the Keys to Forgiveness Scale, KFS, located in Appendix I. The numbers in the scale range from one to ten, and they are defined from slight to extremely difficult to forgive, get over, and move forward. The scale was designed to affirm, acknowledge, and release oneself or anyone over anything in order to not get stuck in our wounds from the past or present. It was to lighten the load, so to speak, in order to run the race set before us to the finish line.

There have been differing degrees of pain or trauma in my life (and possibly your life too), but by placing the event with the individual(s) on this sliding scale, it helped me to understand why some events and people are easier to let go of compared to others. If you are struggling with life events, this scale may help you as well. On a lower scale, I could easily let go, but on a higher scale, it took time to recover and heal. Although, I did forgive on all accounts. That takes grace, and it may also take time. Not everything that happens to us is healed instantly, as we would like it to be. Life can be complicated, but we can overcome all things through Christ who strengthens us. The Bible teaches, "Yet in all these things we are more than conquerors through Him who loved us" (Rom. 8:37).

In this chapter, for instance, the traumatic events rated anywhere from a five up through a ten if I separated them by when they occurred and how they affected me. What matters most is that after acknowledging the painful experience (because I couldn't wish it away, and maybe you can't either), it's important to forgive and release (let go of) those involved and move forward into all that God has in store for us by persevering faith.

As a new Christian or a baby Christian (as some may say), I needed love and grace extended toward me from others, not condemnation or judgment, because it was a rocky road at times. Why? By making poor decisions, I paid a price, and I believe God turned those things around for good in the end. God, above all, is faithful and loving, and His mercy endures forever. He is who I ran to, but He also sent and used other people (such as mentors) along the way. In Appendix II you will find Solutions for Overcoming. These useful tools helped me triumph over adversity, so I included them for easy reference. In the Lord's redemptive process, He deserves the glory for healing and delivering me from the destructive pit of drug abuse and the culture that goes with it. The Psalmist says:

> Who redeems your life from destruction, who crowns you with loving-kindness and tender mercies, who satisfies your mouth with good things, so that your youth is renewed like the eagles. (Ps. 103:4–5)

Here's one final verse: "In truth I perceive that God shows no partiality" (Acts 10:34). Meaning, what He has done for me, likewise, He wants to do for you. His power can set anyone free from their past or the bully, drugs.

CHAPTER 2

MY INFORMATIVE YEARS

Jesus said, "Let the little children come to me, and do not hinder them, for the kingdom of heaven belongs to such as these."
— Matthew 19:14 (New International Version)

In first grade I attended an elementary school in North Carolina. The school was in walking distance from our house, in what I call middle-class suburbia. Initially, when the school counselor tested me for entrance into first grade, I tested on the bright side of the diagnostic exam. That score automatically placed me in a class for exceptional learners, much to my surprise. However, that would not be the only surprise.

With the testing out of the way, it was time to go school shopping, as summer was nearly over. Who wouldn't be eager to shop for a new wardrobe to start the school year off? Just the thought of new clothes and new shoes captivated my attention. We weren't required to wear a uniform, but girls couldn't wear pants either, so that left only dresses, skirts, and pantsuits—no shorts, no midriff shirts, and no jeans, unlike some wear today. Anyhow, Mom and I set out to shop for dresses that were only permitted to fall an inch or two above the knee, no higher. Any higher than that, and we stood being sent home to change. If the temperatures should become frigid as the season went on, we were allowed to wear pantsuits. The pantsuits looked like dresses with pants underneath—go figure. Here again, we couldn't wear pants, only pantsuits. Eventually, that rule changed to allow pants year-round. Certainly, I, for one, was glad to hear about being able to wear pants to school every single day of the year.

When Mom and I first set out to find clothes, I started off the year with a normal BMI for my weight and height. My size at that point was never a concern to anyone. So there's not much I could say yet about my size. Next, being the shoe person that I am today, when it came to shoes on the list back then, I already had my heart set on a pair of Buster Brown shoes. To my amazement, my wish was granted. Those shoes were all the rage in the 1960s. The shoe company featured a comic strip character named Buster and his sidekick, Tige the dog. The now famous duo became the mascots for the company, and the company produced a commercial that was so cute it made you want to wear a pair of their shoes. They must have succeeded in their power of persuasion on their brand because they won me over, puppy and all.

After a day of school shopping, I put all my new belongings away except for my new saddle shoes with the label of Buster Brown and his dog on the inside soles. Those adorable new shoes sat right next to my bed because I couldn't wait to put them on upon waking. I couldn't wait to wear them and break them in. My sister and I were allowed only one pair of new shoes per school year, and we had to take good care of them because they had to last all year long. Now today, I have more than one pair of shoes, and I've definitely made up for the past one-pair-of-shoes-per-school-year rule. All right, enough said about shoes. Once everything was bought and purchased for my first day in school, the dreaded early-to-bed routine began, which was all purpose-driven, mind you, for the school year that lay ahead.

What did lay ahead? A new school, a new classroom with unfamiliar faces, lots of new rules, a longer school day, and a new female teacher who gave us assigned seats. At first, my teacher seemed to bombard us with constant information that was given at an accelerated pace. Incredibly, I found that hectic pace (for a small fry) a bit nerve-racking, and I quickly tried to adjust to the added demands expected of us within a structured classroom. I wasn't ready for the extra pressure or learning at lightning speed. That was my introduction into a highly organized setting of academics.

However, in the classroom adjacent to us, I could hear periodic disturbances and commotion. That noise became a great distraction to learning, as everyone in the room seemed to both freeze and grimace in silence. Of course, we were yearning to know what was going on in the room next-door, although no details were ever explained to us. To me, it appeared the students were always in trouble. Their teacher (I'm so glad it wasn't my teacher) would line everyone up in the hallway and go right down the line, swatting each student using a huge wooden paddle. I could hear the sharp slap of the paddle followed by wailing kids outside our doorway. The intrusive noise would send our teacher quietly over to shut our door to silence the chaotic atmosphere.

Several things upset me as I plainly observed the situation and tried to make sense of the sobbing without having any reasonable explanation. The doors between our two classrooms were not always shut. When one child or several were out of order, all were punished by the teacher next-door. Having never witnessed that type of behavior in my entire young life, it greatly shocked me. My limited rationale and legitimate fears became real concerns: Would my teacher line us up and spank us all in front of everyone? Why were those children being punished in the hallway? What did they do wrong? Their cries and sobs made it hard to concentrate on schoolwork. That, in itself, wasn't an isolated event, but sometimes it happened more or less frequently. Watching that type of treatment in school at six or seven years of age impacted my ability to learn. Over time, my smile for the school year simply faded into that of a sad face, which led my parents to become concerned.

The stress in the classroom also intensified, as we were being taught at hyperspeed. Who could smile? Kids in my class were in trouble too, but we all did not pay the price of the one. Thank goodness. All of that left me with a fear of misbehaving, which led me to think, *I might be treated like that too if I am wrong.* There was also a fear of my teacher's retaliation and a fear of corporal punishment being executed in the hallway. Without any commentary on spanking in the classroom or the hallway, for that matter, a fear of adults gained access to me in elementary school. Bullied by fear or by adults or both?

How can you take young first graders and expect them to excel at hyperspeed under duress? I couldn't. How can you learn in that environment? Who could I tell? Who would listen? We were taught in school and at my house that children should be seen and not heard." That's disheartening. I don't agree. Who invented that type of child rearing back in the sixties? There was no internet for parents to compare beliefs, guidelines, rules, child-rearing techniques, or ethics. Believe it or not, this opinion is still used and referenced online today. The *medieval phrase* originated around 1450 from an Augustinian clergyman and was recorded in a collection of homilies titled "Mirk's Festival." The thought pattern existed to control children—and even women. In the sixties some other statements or rules that were taught included: Do listen and trust adults, and don't question their authority. Do what adults tell you to do, and don't ask why. And be quiet (don't speak) until you're spoken to. Those are some of the sayings that we were expected to obey and not question.

The terms of endearment were not always so dear. At best, they were archaic, and those tactics produced fear, intimidation, and conformity to authority. It didn't matter whether that person was right or wrong. It wasn't inward obedience; rather, it was fear of reprisal if you didn't conform to what was asked. Maybe to adults it looked like obedience when that wasn't always the case.

That legitimate form of indoctrination (back then) brought trouble in my future. Using fear to control children proved to be a poor choice. When children are instructed to always trust adults, listen to what they say, and obey the person in charge, they learn rules that cannot apply to every situation. On the other hand, if you don't teach a child, he or she can become a menace and get into trouble.

If you train up children in the way that they should go and to know the Lord, they can become good sports about life and (hopefully) go on to follow the Lord. But if you abuse children, they will need healing and more. Certainly, some training standards have their place and merits, but on the opposite side of the spectrum, when they're misused, abuse of authority can occur. Unknowingly, that indoctrination set me up to become innocently and naively involved with a pedophile in our neighborhood. Fear of adult punishment became a bully, and misuse of their authority provoked distrust, not love, trust, or safety. Instead, I sat twisting my hair, not permitted to speak up, speak out, or ask why. Honestly, I was full of life and words inside. Maybe I appeared serene on the outside as I twisted my hair and stared into space, speechless and withdrawn. Yet inwardly, I spoke without saying a thing in my imaginary world of make-believe and literal trauma. Now I have my voice and words, and I must edit them—for real. On a side note, the abuse of adult authority set me up in the future to avoid and ignore authority figures, as mistrust in their words or actions toward me grew as I got older.

> The fear of man brings a snare, but whoever trusts in the
> Lord shall be safe. (Prov. 29:25)

Directives such as, "Obey the adult who is with you," "Listen to your elders," and, "Obey your teachers," couldn't be further from the truth when teachers or adults *cross* boundaries. The discussion of personal boundaries was not defined until the mid-1980s. So without any established etiquette in place like healthy boundaries, I am sure I wasn't the only child who was misguided by similar teachings. Propaganda like the above was misleading because it stopped internal intuition or listening to one's inner self for protection. Even if I felt threatened, I complied with the requests of the adults in charge. Any inner bells going off in my mind became muzzled and confusing. I complied as directed and expected.

There weren't any warning signs (or red flags) discussed that could alert me to stranger danger back then. Due to that fact, I learned to bury my emotions, discrediting any creditable feelings. All of which lay dormant inside my head—as a nondisclosed plea in the future. That philosophy in raising a child to always be quiet and obey adults haunted me on more than one occasion while growing up. Years later it dawned on me what an incorrect teaching had been passed down for generations. Even the Bible says in Psalms 118:8, "It is better to trust in the Lord than to put confidence in man." Although that era no longer exists, the teachings have survived time, as it still remains a stumbling block on the internet today.

PRIVATE SCHOOL

By the end of that first year in public school, my grandmother and parents could tell I was sad—no joke. I was afraid to go to school, and they became concerned. Nobody asked me what was wrong, but they could see it on my sad, little face. A few years later, my grandmother shared with me: "Everyone knew something was wrong because you stopped smiling and lost weight."

In the future, my skinny body was going to drastically change, which would usher in a new type of bullying: being bullied for being overweight. However, at that point in time, my rational skills and verbal abilities weren't fully developed. I was too young to communicate effectively on abnormal adult behavior. So how could I explain what was wrong when every adult was always right? I was constantly being told what to do, told to be quiet, told not to talk back, and told not to ask questions. Back in the day, you did what was asked, and you couldn't question any adults' authority. Plus, it was forbidden to argue back no matter what the circumstance. If you did, you risked being swatted or punished for talking back and not doing what you were told, and you did it without any explanation as to why you were asked to do it. What was permissible to say in return of a demand or command or a rule? Not much back then outside of being polite, remaining courteous, and using proper manners.

My words were all bottled up inside on behalf of my own defense. Here's what I wanted to say but simply couldn't: "I don't want to go to school because they line you up out in the hallway and smack you with a large wooden paddle with holes in it. Everyone's crying in the hall, and nobody smiles. I'm too afraid of being spanked when I did nothing wrong at school. I'm afraid of the teacher in the next room. And there's more ..." However, that's not what came out of my mouth. Little to nothing came out of my mouth to explain my sad face. Yet, by the end of the summer, school would indeed change for the following year.

Back in the sixties, the advocates of corporal punishment saw their protocol as normal and acceptable. No reason or phone call was ever necessary to the parent of a child. From my vantage point, I don't accept how that was handled without informing and involving all concerned parties. Physical punishment was standard procedure for wrongdoing in school while I was growing up, *but abuse of authority is unacceptable.* True boundaries and rights were not clearly defined or questioned as they are today in order to protect children from harm. Now, people can record with a smartphone any perpetrator who loses their temper and misrepresents a child by abusing their authority. For others like me, they are silent no more.

Finally, there was a way out of my public-school dilemma. My parents started attending a new church, and that church was opening their first private school. Everyone must have thought that was the answer to the problem, and it became my parents' heartfelt desire to "Train up a child in the way he should go, and when he is old, he will not depart from it" (Prov. 22:6). We were a young Christian family with a desire to learn about and serve the Lord. So with the grand opening of the new building, my parents enrolled both my sister and I into a private Christian school. *But* nobody truly knew how the rules of engagement would be enforced at that private school either. Were children ever meant to talk and learn how to communicate? Unconceivably, that was all I knew in my tiny world, and I was in for a rude awakening upon switching from a public to a private school system. If I thought the former school was troublesome, the latter proved to be a mixture of good and incredibly harmful. Sorry to say—and I wish I didn't have to say—again, I wasn't prepared for what awaited me. This left me somewhat excited and somewhat reserved, as I started off with great expectations—you know, a brand-new start and a fresh beginning.

Disclaimer: Without a doubt, not all schools, past, present, or future, fall under a category in bullying. See the introduction for an exhaustive definition on bullying. In spite of it all, the good, the bad, and the ugly, I was taught the Word of God in church, in school, and at home. Besides, it became important to separate what is of the Lord and what isn't and to hold on to the good and let go of the ugly. God is good. His Word doesn't return back void, but it will accomplish what it is sent out to do in our lives. In the end, knowing Bible verses produced fruit, brought healing, and set a captive free—me. He replaced pain with overcoming victory. It is His Word I hid in my heart and hung onto all these years. Plus, I forgave and let go of the irregular, maladjusted human stuff, whether it took place in a public or private school system. (See Isaiah 55:11, Isaiah 61:1, Psalms 119:11, and Galatians 5:22–23.)

THE LEARNING CURVE

However, the rules at that Christian school proved to be worse in comparison to what I had experienced the year before. Certainly, the new changes caught me off guard. How could my parents know what I was going to face? They wouldn't have known. As antiquated as this might sound, I was still part of an age where a physical ruler could be smacked across your hands in school. I had never witnessed that type of abuse, and while looking into it, I read that such abuse can affect an individual for more than thirty years.

The rules at that new school were so rigid, so controlling, and, I realize now, so uncalled for and abusive, that it's no wonder I was afraid to speak out loud. This was especially true after watching the knuckles and palms of a few students being hit in the classroom in front of everyone. Was that normal adult behavior? Was that the norm everywhere? I would not know the answer to that question for years.

To top it off, students were not allowed to talk in school. The only place a student could converse was at recess. I don't recall any chatter going on while eating lunch, and we all sat at attention during this time. That must have been how passing notes in school (before cell phones and texting) evolved in the future—because we couldn't talk to each other. In the hallway, students walked in formation as they filed by other classrooms. Everyone was to form a single line within an arm's length of the person in front of you (and you couldn't touch them), just like marching in the military. Everyone walked as a group in formation and stopped in line as a group, and you could never be caught talking or touching anyone while in line, or you were removed from the group and paddled.

While in class, you could never speak a word or ask a question unless you raised your hand and were asked or called upon. Well, I understand the raise your hand part, but the no talking part showed up everywhere I went. Sometimes you weren't called on when you had a need, and your hand was raised up high. What if it was a valid need? There you had to sit like a toad in hot water being ignored. What if you had to go to the bathroom? Both schools made going to the bathroom a major issue, so much so that I had wet my pants on more than one occasion after being denied or being told to, "Go back to your chair and sit down and wait." Talk about embarrassing. It wasn't only me. There were others too.

Many times, I had a urinary tract infection needing a doctor's visit and, consequently, medication. Finally, a note was written for me from home just to pee, given the urgency to void and to avoid another UTI. That made my mom furious at them and that she had to write a note so I could pee when necessary. How crazy is that? The other inconsolable part was that I had surgery when I was small regarding UTIs, followed by further testing as a growing child. Had it been known, those were difficult events and memories to forget. So needless to say, I meant it when I raised my hand or asked to leave and was not looking for an excuse to get me out of the classroom (like I did when I was a teenager). Just the thought of it all makes me cringe.

Another rule was that you could not get out of your seat and walk anywhere—for example, to sharpen your pencil or even to walk up to the teacher's desk and ask for help. You couldn't talk to your neighbor sitting beside you in class either. You did exactly as you were told, which included sitting up straight and at attention at all times. Good posture is wonderful, but sitting straight as a board is not easy as a young child. If you dropped an eraser on the floor beside your chair, you couldn't just bend over to pick it up because you risked getting into trouble when you bent down to reach for it. I watched it happen to others. In fear, one time I swiftly bent over to pick up my pencil when it fell on the floor during a test. I was afraid of being punished in front of the whole class. I wasn't sure if I should ask to pick up my pencil or if I could innocently pick it up. What a learning curve to abide by in elementary school. It seemed like nobody smiled in school, except maybe at recess. Rules, obedience, structure, and discipline are all important (so please don't read me wrong here), but when they are taken out of context, they can become excessive and abusive. The hope is to raise healthy minded children, not functional robots.

The misuse of authority and fear-based control were part of the educational process during my elementary years. To this day, I recall the principal entering the classroom and placing a young boy from our class in front of all the students. As the principal stood right next to him, he began to whack the student with a thick wooden board in front of the entire class. The punishment continued until the student submitted to what was asked of him—namely, to be quiet. At first the swats made him laugh in his awkwardness, like a protective mechanism in front of everyone. The young boy didn't know what was coming by the look in his eyes. His eyes were as big as saucers. It was a surprise to him *and* us. And the swats continued unabated. The class was already dead silent. Still, nobody even flinched a muscle. As the students faced the boy, the awkward giggles begat continued lickings until the child finally broke down and cried … his spirit now broken. Only then did the principal stop, and the child was separated from a room filled with horrified, speechless children.

Without a doubt, I was terrified by what I witnessed, so much so that I could have wet my pants, but my thoughts and emotions froze up inside instead. That left me both alarmed and upset, yet I dare not say word. We dare not speak. I couldn't articulate that sudden cruel demeanor stemming from our principal—our authority figure. I also don't recall the student's behavior ever becoming loud or insubordinate inside of the classroom. After that atrocity, I never saw the young boy again, as he was withdrawn from the school system. By whom, I'll never know, but I'm guessing the parents enrolled him elsewhere after that sudden display of abuse. Whether past or present, this is where forgiveness, healing, and restoration come into play with true stories such as these, not only back then but now.

Obviously, certain rules were misaligned in that school, as well as some ethics. In the sixties, corporal punishment in school was advocated, as I mentioned earlier. It was permissible throughout all fifty states. Today, it is banned in thirty-one states. What that principal did back in the day left a mark beyond skin. On the other hand, if that happened in this day and age, the principal and the teachers would have been fired and left to face the judicial system. Now, an incident such as the one I described can not only be seen on the evening news but also on social media. Group bullying in the classroom used to enforce strict rules by others harmed us. At times, the expectation was to conform to their measuring stick or be whipped by it. Group bullying produced more than just fear in us. Thankfully, God can heal *any* memory where fear or abuse has reared its ugly head. Nothing is too hard for God to heal and restore—big or small, past or present.

> Fathers, do not provoke or irritate or fret your children [do not be hard on them or harass them], lest they become discouraged and sullen and morose and feel inferior and frustrated. [Do not break their spirit.] (Col. 3:21 Amplified Bible, Classic Edition)

Yet, while in elementary school, on a much smaller human scale, I was bullied on the bus ride to and from school, but nothing like today. Bill was the first boy to bully me, and we were close in age. We rode the same school bus. Were his actions a silly childhood crush? Maybe, but I doubt that. He always seemed to pick on me. He did everything from repeatedly poking my back (which hurt) to squirting the juice from an orange in my eyes. Once he yanked so hard on my new coat that the belt ripped away from the coat. I was in tears over my ruined blue (fake) fur coat. The belt was torn and couldn't be repaired, and I still wore the now-ugly blue coat to school. Wherever I went, there he was, ready to annoy me. Eventually, Bill was placed on another bus just to keep us separated, which made me all too happy and relieved. On a side note, no one could hit, yell, chew gum, or eat on the bus. Those were obvious rules. There was also no talking on the bus, which was a less obvious rule, but that rule seemed to appear everywhere I went. Nonetheless, it sounds trite to say I was bullied on the bus. It sounds trite compared to today when there is hostile fighting and even weapons being brought on the bus to school.

IN CONCLUSION

As a child in the midst of a grown-up world, some of those experiences were overpowering and distressing to hear or see. Yet, outside of my story being recounted, today you can see injustice being replayed through a quick upload on someone's phone to any broadcasting network. Almost instantly, you can witness children who have been slammed into walls, thrown onto floors, or shoved into lockers, and some have even been locked behind secret walls. I know there is a God who sees and knows and hears their cries. Whether those events stem from the past, are happening right now, or will happen further on down the road, the need remains the same: Jesus. He is our source, our go-to, and our friend in times of need. He can help someone get back on their feet again, bring comfort to the oppressed, and cure the broken places in our minds and hearts over *anything* we've suffered through.

> Behold, the Lord's hand is not shortened, that it cannot save; nor His ear heavy, that it cannot hear.
>
> — Isaiah 59:1

CHAPTER 3

BULLIED FOR BEING FAT AND REJECTED

Faith doesn't always mean that God changes your situation. Sometimes it means He changes you.
— Steven Furtick

By third grade, I began to put weight on my tiny frame, and I was still enrolled in private school. Was it stress eating, or was it my food choices? To some, I appeared a bit plump in third grade, and to others I looked chunky, or so I was told. By the time I reached sixth grade, I was seriously on my way from looking chubby to becoming completely overweight and even obese (and I was told that too). The labels *fat* and *porky* were also used countless times while I was growing up. Those descriptions, among other offensive words, were used to describe me to my face. In my young mind, hearing years of fat-shaming words echo in my head left me feeling ashamed and depressed about myself, except for nobody openly discussed those terms or how they felt. Nor could I use an emoji, as there were no emojis. Regardless, I wouldn't have known any different. I just knew that people did not like the way I looked. Yet in the future, in a moment of time, I would walk away healed.

My grandmother nicknamed me Pumpkin. Deep down, I hated the name and cringed inside when she said it, but I never told her, "That nickname hurts me every time I hear it." I now believe she innocently called me Pumpkin, but at the time, I was thinking, *She's calling me pumpkin because I look like one!* In the future, to hide my embarrassment, I began to grab a pillow off the couch to cover my ever-growing stomach.

My rationale behind the pillow became, "If anyone should walk into the room, I've hid my tummy from view so that my weight will not become part of the conversation (again)." And that is exactly what was happening. My subliminal hopes became, "Will this pillow make my belly disappear from the eyes of others so they won't bully me anymore? If I can hide my stomach, possibly people will stop calling me names." I was just too young to understand that I was trying to protect myself from further body-shaming, even if I was leaning toward becoming obese. That meant others were making fun of the way I looked to them and tearing me down for getting that way. It was not right—not good at all or helpful. Body-shaming and fat-shaming are in a league of their own—completely unacceptable. And besides, mocking me for my size and how big I'd become didn't help in the least. It did not inspire me one iota to lose any weight whatsoever. Instead, I felt that I was a terrible, horrible, no-good person. In other words, my self-esteem was at an all-time low.

Ironically, Mom chose the food we ate. She provided what she thought was not only a fast meal to prepare but also a nutritious one. Yet in the end, those food choices made me heavier, and overall, the meals were not as nutritious as we were led to believe. The advantage was that the preprepared, processed food choices saved time in preparation and were easy to fix. Plus, they became all the rage back then, which added to their appeal. The prepackaged instant and highly processed foods replaced quality nutrition, and the commercials on television about those brands were everywhere.

The growth of the fast-food industry was booming, and they were always coming out with something new. The quick-to-prepare box-to-table foods socked pounds on me, and I craved the food we ate. It was all I knew as I was growing up. These foods included Kellogg's Pop-Tarts, Lucky Charms, Chef Boyardee, Rice-A-Roni, and Hamburger Helper. We ate breakfast in a box, lunch from a can, and dinner from a frozen box or can, all washed down with Nesquik, Kool-Aid, Tang, or Pepsi. I'm sure Mom felt that she was providing us with some of the best foods on the market at the time, like Wonder Bread. My sister and I loved Wonder Bread, especially loaded with peanut butter and jelly. The famous commercial slogan told us Wonder Bread, "Helps build strong bodies twelve ways." Later, it became a controversial government battle and declared a false advertisement in the end, but not at first. Until then, we enjoyed every slice of bread.

On the other hand, we did have home-cooked, made-from-scratch meals too, mostly on Sundays. With the dawn of the fast-food empire laden with fake hydrogenated fats, bleached salts, sugars, and processed flours, I became addicted to eating. There were times I gorged myself with food. One helping was not enough. Sometimes I had two or three helpings, and there were mornings (when nobody was looking) that I gulped down four or more bowls of cereal or three deliciously coated margarine and brown-sugared cinnamon toast. For as young as I was, I turned into a real glutton. The food went beyond reality. It tasted good, smelled great, and made me feel happy. Unknowingly, I self-soothed with food. Candy tasted great and made me smile as I chewed on Milk Duds, M&Ms, and gooey Milky Way candy bars.

When summer arrived, I always managed to find money for when the ice cream truck rolled around. And, as the saying goes, "We all screamed for ice cream," including me, but I screamed the loudest. I had to get my hands on either an ice cream sandwich, fudgesicle, or orange Dreamsicle. On and on the list of edible goodies went. Mom bought the food, and yes, I consumed it. The yummy food backfired in my face one day when she turned around and called me two-ton Tilley. Furthermore, what did that name mean? I certainly had no idea. I couldn't look online. I could only guess, but I was afraid to guess. All the while, Mom blamed and shamed me for gaining weight on food she bought—go figure.

But before I delve into all of this, know it is hard to talk about your own mother, whom I loved, especially when it comes to opening up about painful topics. I would love to paint her in a perfect world, but life isn't and wasn't always perfect. I took care of her before she passed away, and honestly, I didn't fully understand all of what I was getting myself into before her diagnosis and aftercare. Yet I believe that I did the *best* I could do for her until the end. It really hurts to talk about her, as with any loved one, given that I am sharing some of the messy stuff. She wasn't always unfair and hard to deal with. On the other hand, it took grace, forgiveness, and love to conquer all, along with God's healing touch inside my mind and heart as I witnessed her last breath before heaven.

FAT-SHAMING

During my youth, I steadily climbed the scale. At the same time, I had a huge desire to take ballet. There was such a strong passion burning inside me for that beautiful artform. My parents had bought me several books on ballet, and they fueled the desire within me to dance and wear that little black leotard with pink ballet slippers. Excitedly, I inquired about taking ballet and repeatedly asked to take classes. Mother was vehement about me not taking ballet; she would take one stern look at me and shake her head no. It didn't seem to matter how many times I asked for the opportunity to dance, the answer was still no. Instead, she insisted I take piano lessons. What I wanted or thought was never considered in the equation. It wasn't about not having money for classes; that I could understand if she had decided to explain it to me, although having an explanation rarely, if ever, happened.

Playing the piano was what she loved to do, and it was what she wanted me to do too. Mom was an exceptional concert pianist, able to play full concertos from memory. She also skillfully taught others how to play the piano by the age of fourteen and was awarded a full scholarship to an esteemed conservatory of music. She adamantly insisted that I learn to play the piano, no matter how I felt about it—that didn't count. Our Baldwin piano, which (unavoidably) sat in the living room, became a source of ongoing contention between the two of us.

I used to ask, "Why can't I take ballet? I love ballet! Why must I learn to play the piano?"

Then, out of the blue, while Mom was sitting on the piano bench next to me, she abruptly turned around and slapped me across the face. And it wasn't a soft slap either. That more than startled me; it stunned me, as I was trying to stay focused and learn a new piano lesson. Then, she persisted with, "You *will* learn to play the piano correctly—period." After that sudden, surprise slap across the face, it was over for me (inwardly). I quit. But, of course, I didn't say that. Instead, I made piano days miserable for both of us in a passive-aggressive sort of way. Finally, she gave up on the idea that I was to become a concert pianist like her.

Mom originally told me, "I gave up a scholarship and college in order to get married and have babies." So quite possibly, she missed playing the piano so much that she wanted me to carry on her passion for playing the piano. I'm not sure. I just knew the desire to play was not inside my head.

Ballet was the dream inside my head. I yearned to dance, yet Mom would say, "How could such a chubby little girl be seen on stage in a tutu?" She saw me as roly-poly, which meant she saw me rolling across the stage versus the pirouettes I envisioned inside my head, crushing my dreams and crushing me. She continued to say no to my repeated requests to dance, rather reciting, "You're too big to be seen on stage. That's all I'll hear about from others—how heavy you are."

I endured many fat-shaming talks in private by my own mother. Fat-shaming or body-shaming means that someone is telling a child (me) or an adult that he or she is too fat in a derogatory, demeaning way. But those two terms weren't used when I was young as they are today. It hurt even more what was being said behind closed doors, and I never told anyone for years. Besides, I was repeatedly told, "You're not to tell anybody what goes on inside our house. What is said in our house, stays in our house. You're not to tell the neighbors anything we discuss." So instead, I buried the pain and embarrassment. But in the far future, I did tell someone—a therapist. It's hard to admit whatever was said or done, but I worked through, forgave, and let go of every unkind word or action from others and from my own mother. Rather, I let go of the labels and the emotional abuse. And I thank God that He can heal anyone where it hurts the most.

However, I wasn't quick to forget that slap across the face while growing up or my internal desire to dance. The slap on the face stung my emerging ego, snatching away my confidence, in addition to all the ridicule I endured. I was unable to speak up to my mom, as the following phrase was endorsed: Children are to be seen and not heard. Plus, I wasn't allowed to speak up; that was interpreted as "talking back" which you were not permitted to do under any circumstance. So I just buried the hurt inside and ate away my pain. Boy, I loved those Hostess Cupcakes and HoHos, followed by Little Debbie Nutty Bars and Oatmeal Creme Pies, which were created in the sixties. The sweets soothed unresolved conflicts and anger that I had toward my mother, and besides, they were delectable. Perhaps had I taken ballet, I may have lost the extra weight. I'm just saying it's possible. Instead, I put on more weight and continued to be bullied for being heavy at home and at school.

The conflicts at home often led my parents to argue about me being overweight. My father tried to rescue me from my mom who was fat-shaming me along with calling me two-ton Tilly. Honestly, I really didn't like being called that name (and who would), and I didn't know the meaning of the saying, but I surmised it meant a tremendously large person, meaning me. Only by searching the internet today did I find out what that phrase actually meant. It was the title of a song written in 1956 of a man describing how obese his lady friend had become. I was amazed to hear the meaning of the name and the fact that it turned into a song. I'm very glad she didn't sing it to me, so the lyrics would replay again and again in my head. Anyhow, my parents yelled back-and-forth about my size. Of course, their yelling made me feel more than horrible about myself, as I ran to my bedroom to cry and eat because of the emotional upheaval taking place inside our house over me. Due to that, I secretly kept extra food stashed in a dresser drawer. Just to avoid being openly reprimanded while eating, so I could devour the goodies. Thereby, I became a secret binge eater and food hoarder even before those words were in vogue. By the way, as of 2013, binge eating is now considered a diagnostic disorder: binge eating disorder, or BED. Back then, those terms weren't discussed or labeled as such. Despite that fact, while growing up, my motive behind hiding food was, "If no one can see me eat, I can't get yelled at for eating. Then my parents won't argue in front of me or behind my back," which echoed throughout the house and in my head. Hiding food to eat led me to avoid hearing their arguments and also realizing how much I was actually eating, which added to their fuss and fumes over me too. That is how I turned into a secret binge eater or an emotional eater, as some may say, by fifth grade. And I'd like to add that the Lord healed me of why I used to overeat and hide food. He healed me of the root cause of my binging alongside the memories that held me captive for so long, so it wasn't just about food; there was more to it.

By sixth grade, I remember my parents telling me, "You're now at the age to join in adult conversations." Well, how completely odd and foreign that sounded to my ears. I could now talk with adults! Where were my words? I must go and find them. Before that, I had to be quiet in a room full of adults, or I was asked to leave the room, stay in the basement and play, and not interrupt for any reason. I was eleven or twelve and recall thinking, *Wow, I can talk now! And I don't even know what to say!* That dogma inbred inside me seemed to follow me wherever I went while growing up. So I've deemed them the *silent years*; now they're behind me. Not only is that in the past, but when I was older, I took to the stage in dance, in theater, and on television. They were small television parts, but hey, I'm glad I did it. I found my voice and my ballet shoes (yes, even pointe shoes) later in life. And it was worth it in the end. When that creative season in life arrived, it was more than liberating. "Yet in all these things we are more than conquerors through Him who loved us" (Rom. 8:37).

MORE FOODIES

Also, when I was a tween, my parents reenrolled my sister and I back into public school after four years of private schooling. That meant I returned to the same school I transferred out of in elementary school, the one that paddled an entire classroom in the hallway. But also by sixth grade, I'd become the heaviest I've ever been. Was it my secret binge eating? I had a personal interest in cooking and baking and learned to cook and bake by the age of ten. Then, while everyone was watching television, I would sneak into the kitchen and stuff my face with my very own baked goods during commercials with the hopes that I would not get caught. In an *all-purpose* world of Betty Crocker, the Pillsbury Doughboy, Oscar Mayer, not to forget Kraft Macaroni and Cheese, and Kenner's Easy-Bake Oven, I ate until I was bursting at the seams, literally.

That meant red tear marks and dimples began to show up all over my preteen body. Eventually, the marks became pink and then a creamy white. They're called stretchmarks—just another secret I kept hidden from view. It wasn't until the sixties that the word *cellulite* came into print inside of periodicals and journals. That would describe my dimples down to a tee. But I would not have known about that definition back then. As a youth, I only sought to hide it all, as I felt that ashamed about myself. Those embarrassing, unsightly marks blossomed on my preadolescent body, and I was extremely self-conscious of them. When the summer heat soared and short shorts were in style, along with bikini season, everyone dressed for the temperature except for me. Short shorts and swimwear became the last thing I wanted to put on or be seen in. Most of all, I was concerned that people might see my stretchmarks and make fun of me for having them.

The cause and effect of overeating and lack of exercise was wearing on me. Sitting around and watching too much television versus running outside to play in the neighborhood took away my energy as I put on more weight. When my sister and I were alone, she became my personal errand girl. Instead of getting up to get my own snack or something to do, I would yell for my thin sister to come and then ask her to bring things to me. Which she was happy to oblige, while I sat on the couch in front of the television and indulged myself with snacks. Sis was active, and I was a pure couch potato. The comparison from other people over the two of us became: "Your sister looks like a beanpole, and you look, well ... plumper."

What preyed on my mind was a reclusive thought life of feeling terrible about myself over the weight I gained (on top of being compared to my thinner sister). And for that reason, I went on a search inside the house for a remedy—more so, a quick fix. That search led me to find and then devour the little chocolate squares called Ex-Lax. Please don't laugh out loud. I actually thought I would lose weight by eating them. You were only to eat one or two of the little squares, which looked like the chocolate squares from a Hershey's Milk Chocolate Bar, but they weren't. And they didn't taste like Hershey's chocolate. Ex-Lax is a laxative, and I seriously thought more was better. *Not.* They are not candy! But, my young self wanted to see if they would help me to shed a few pounds. Besides, I found them in the medicine cabinet, and they belonged to Mom. So they must be OK. Well, I'm not sure how many I ate, but in the end, I didn't even shed an ounce.

Regardless, the family arguments continued over my weight gain. I could hear my parents shouting in the background or right in front of me and through the vents on the floor in my room. My mother would yell at me for eating. In return, my father ran to my defense, saying, "Stop picking on her." She would yell back, "You're always defending her. You always run to her rescue." Yet Mom bought the food we ate. That pattern of arguing about my size only perpetuated as I morphed into self-soothe mode because I felt I caused all the family arguments, and I also felt wholeheartedly responsible. Talk about not liking yourself. ... No, in the future, talk about God healing a person's self-image.

Soon, I developed a wheat allergy that nobody knew about, or maybe it was always there, I'll never know. Yet, no one in my family discussed allergies. My poor stomach was always nauseous, which led my mother to take me to visit a doctor to have my stomach checked with the hopes of finding a reason. Even while visiting the doctor, he never found anything wrong with me upon examination, and he never once tested me for any food allergies. He did conduct an x-ray, but having seen nothing lodged inside my stomach, he dismissed me and sent us on our way to purchase over-the-counter remedies.

To compensate for the upset stomach, I consumed large quantities of Maalox, TUMS, and Rolaids. That's what I lived on besides Pepto-Bismol and Milk of Magnesia. For years (and years to come), those were my go-to medicines. Ironically, that was the antidote the doctor told us to use. The meds brought some relief but not a cure. At the time, food allergies and diagnostics were not on the doctor's horizon, and the means to find out were not readily available where we lived years ago. Furthermore, we never discussed any allergy during our visit. Back then, gluten sensitivity, gluten intolerance, and celiac disease were not considered a cause for stomach ailments, but the criteria would one day become established in the far-off future. Gluten (an allergen) was in almost everything I ate—go figure. The symptomatology and tests for CD were not clearly defined, and although they existed, it wasn't until 1990 that new and acceptable diagnostic guidelines were universally established and accepted worldwide. That extremely delayed information was comforting to know years later, as some may say, better late than never. And yet, who would have guessed that by eliminating gluten, my stomach would be healed? But, one day it came to pass.

Until then, the lack of knowledge left me to eat my favorite breakfast cereals. Cereal, to me, was like a famous Lay's Potato Chip saying: "Betcha can't eat just one!" For a fact, I couldn't eat just one bowl of Lucky Charms, Cocoa Krispies, or Sugar Frosted Flakes; it was more like four or five bowls of Corn Pops and Captain Crunch. Remember eating those growing up? Not to forget Kellogg's Pop-Tarts, my favorite being Frosted Brown Sugar Cinnamon and Chocolate Fudge. Remember those? They still exist!

Anyhow, after consuming my favorites, I would vomit on the school bus when I use to take a bus to school. The bus driver actually kept extra barf bags on the bus for me to grab, if I felt I was going to puke. And then, there were times I made it through the knee-jerk bus ride only to arrive at school to rush inside the nearest bathroom to puke my brains out. I know that sounds gross. Sorry. Really, who can eat that much processed cereal? Unbelievably, I could! Plus, I had no idea I had an allergy. And incredibly, the bus captain rerouted the bus to pick me up last and drop me off first. Just so I wouldn't vomit on his bus. Had the allergy been discovered, I may have had an entirely different bus ride experience to and from school.

Yet another time after school was out, I was busy playing across the street with my girlfriend. The game we liked to play was called tetherball. We were having a terrific time swinging the ball back-and-forth on the cord to see who could shove the ball the hardest and wrap the cord around the pole to win. That was the object of the game. To pull that off, you had to overpower your opponent by taking control of the ball. Once you had control of the ball, then you forcefully tried to wrap the cord around the pole as fast as you could without the ball being intercepted, and whoever could do that was the winner. But in the background (as if I had no ears) I could hear the neighbors (all adults) out on their porches discussing my size as if I were invisible. But I wasn't. They began to openly discuss how huge I looked (and that wasn't the word they used, but you get the idea). Maybe to them they were talking behind my back, you know—gossiping—like I wasn't there, but I could hear them perfectly. When suddenly, my face turned bright red, as I felt completely and emphatically annihilated in front of everyone present.

Not only was I stunned by grown-ups talking about how obese I was becoming, along with even more undesirable adjectives, but the person who instigated the entire conversation was also morbidly obese. I would never have treated that adult in like manner. It took a lot of nerve for the neighbor who had weight issues to single me out in front of everyone and publicly shame me for my size. Of course, that wasn't nice or fair for a child to hear. However, life is not fair all the time, is it? "And besides they learn to be idle, wandering about from house to house, and not only idle but also gossips and busybodies, saying things which they ought not" (1 Tim. 5:13). Quickly, because of all that was said, I dropped the game in front of my girlfriend, due to the fact I was overcome and embarrassed by their bullying. Immediately, I ran home with my heart on my sleeve and tears in my eyes from being the brunt end of their adult jokes. And still, I held my mouth shut (when I was going to pieces on the inside) and didn't speak up for myself against a group of adults. As I was told growing up, "You don't talk back to adults."

In the future, and as a Christian, I took the high road and forgave the ones who tore me down because I wanted all that God had instore for me. In Jeremiah 29:11 it says, "For I know the thoughts that I think toward you, says the Lord, thoughts of peace and not of evil, to give you a future and a hope."

MY FIRST CRUSH

Despite it all, I had a crush on a boy at school, and I liked him. At the same time, that is when bullying before, during, and after school began. All because I liked someone. Honestly, he was my first crush. And where did he live? He lived on my street (of all things), and everything was fine until he found out I was attracted to him. When he heard about my crush, he never let me forget it. He never let me forget that I said, "I think he's cute," that I said, "I really like him." Afterward, my childhood crush called me every fat-shamming name in the book, the rudest and the cruelest kind of names. The kind of names, that make you cry on the inside if not on the outside too.

And not only then, but today these types of labels are passed around and pasted everywhere on social media streams or sent as a group text to an individual's cell phone, thereby hurting that person. Take the word *blubbo*, for instance. That word was screamed out loud at me more times than I can put into print. It felt, to me, like a horrific social media firestorm because it didn't go away overnight. The offense was repeated again and again. I couldn't hit a delete button or block my caller or get a new phone (as these choices didn't exist). I couldn't move away from it all (like I owned my home; I was still a child, really a tween, mind you). My childhood crush didn't just say rotten words to my face. The infamous labels echoed throughout the school halls and in the neighborhood (for all ears to hear) and in my head. He would deliberately go on a verbal rampage, making fun of me until I ran or walked away as fast as I could to and from school. Lunch and recess became such an emotional disaster zone that I ended up going home to eat lunch by myself. Sometimes I never returned to finish the day at school (and nobody knew or asked). That was to avoid being harassed in public at school, not only by him but also by his group of friends who joined in the antics. Their words tormented me, as I heard them constantly. Every day for what seemed like years, Randy, as I'll call him, yelled loudly, so loud I bet the whole world could hear (at least it felt like the entire universe could hear). I couldn't seem to escape his bullying or, for that matter, all of their bullying over my size.

Yet, in the future, something or someone bullied Randy to the point that he took his own life in high school. Well, I did hear of what happened to him, but I'll never know why he did what he did. That was shocking news to find out, as bullying wasn't a local or national or international topic like it is today. Also, high school suicide rates were extremely low nationally in the seventies and varied from coast to coast. In high school, never once did I hear of suicide prevention being discussed. And I never heard of anyone else taking his own life in school. Currently, suicide ranks as the tenth leading cause of death in the United States overall. And sadly, because bullying has increased, there has been an increased risk of suicidal ideation, suicide attempts, and completed suicide, according to several national organizations. The wounds created from being a victim of bullying (whether young or old) can be healed and restored. Know the Lord has a destiny for you and for me, and it's not suicide. Suicide is not an option or the answer. The Lord is!

> What then shall we say to these things? If God is for us,
> who can be against us? (Rom. 8:31)

So, when Randy and his friends started to make fun of me for being overweight, the group in and of itself scared me, on top of the name-calling, because they were classmates and neighborhood friends. They really were not true friends to begin with, as my real friend group was getting smaller and smaller all the time. And those friends didn't abandon me or treat me disrespectfully for being a plus size. Not only did I feel tormented like I had said, but I was also petrified of Randy and his group. Once Randy knew I liked him, he set out to make doubly sure that I would quit liking him. Of course, I quit liking him. Right away, I quit liking him, and I tried to stay away from him and his friends entirely. The pursuit of the kids against me left me feeling not only harassed but distraught and sullen, more so depressed. And, ironically, I wouldn't have known that I was depressed. That vocabulary word was never used inside my world back in the day. Maybe sad, yes; only I never told anyone about those experiences. Rather, I kept them to myself and buried them inside.

Anyhow, telling Randy how I liked him was unforeseeably regrettable. None of which helped my underdeveloped self-confidence or self-esteem, if there was anything left by then. Such rejection caused me to withdraw into silence from those in my own neighborhood, sorry to say. I wasn't looking to be shunned or rejected, and both caught me quite off guard. Although, one day those emotions and memories would be forever healed and lost in time. Back then, playtime in the neighborhood was reduced to only a few chosen girlfriends. Due to the ongoing commotion, I ended up avoiding certain houses on both sides of our street, and I never went near Randy's house (because he would yell obscenities out his window if he saw me). So to protect myself while playing, I purposefully rode my bike completely around the block to avoid his house on the corner, because Randy would spare nothing if he saw me passing by.

As you can read, my first crush ended abruptly. Nonetheless, I did survive being bullied by Randy, his friends, as well as others, while they shouted throughout the neighborhood and at school. But that's not to say it didn't wreck me. Today social bullying has grown exponentially. Likewise, it is being talked about everywhere, and back then, it was rarely mentioned. Not only are words being hollered throughout social media forums for all ears to hear and eyes to watch, but it then travels around the world in a matter of minutes via the internet. Everyone sees it, some experience it, but it's never too late to be healed from the pain of malicious words, actions, or labels. God can heal the brokenness that words or cruel actions have left behind.

IN CONCLUSION

Perhaps the best story that emerged from these stories on being bullied over my size came much later. Truly the best was yet to come. And that happened when the Lord healed me of rejection, fear, and any abuse I endured at home, at school, or in the neighborhood. Whether it was the way I looked, what I wore, what I tried to say, or what I could not say, He restored me. No matter what was said to me that brought about woundedness, left scars, or caused gaping holes, the Lord saw inside my heart. He saw the mess, and He can heal messes!

Years later, just before I left for college, I attended an outdoor Christian festival. It was the kind of festival where you pitch a tent or park your camper, and then you set up camp and hang out with new acquaintances and old friends, making new memories. The yearly Christian festivals (which are still ongoing today) combine Christian contemporary music (CCM) alongside anointed teachers and pastors from all over the United States and beyond.

It was at one of those festivals where I heard a preacher speaking on rejection, and toward the end of his message he said, "God wants to heal anyone who has experienced rejection in their life." Rejection is just one byproduct of bullying. So it was there inside of a crowded tent, that I cried out to the Lord, and He heard me. Right then, right there, I forgave everyone who had ever hurt me. It was the Lord in His mighty power that set out to set me free. He delivered me from the hold their words had upon my mind and thought life (holding me captive). In Psalms 34:17 it says, "The righteous cry out, and the Lord hears, and delivers them out of all their troubles." And if rejection, stemming from abuse or bullying has hurt you deeply and robbed you of the unique person that you are, know that the Lord can heal and restore you. (It's never too late.) Thereby, turning your mourning into dancing once again.

"I shall not die, but live, and declare the works of the Lord.
— Psalms 118:17

There is therefore now no condemnation to those who are in Christ Jesus, who do not walk according to the flesh, but according to the Spirit.

— Romans 8:1

CHAPTER 4

MY YOUTH DESTROYED

Focus on giants—you stumble. Focus on God—Giants tumble.

— Max Lucado

Plain and simple, I had a fear of getting into trouble every time I thought of communicating to my parents regarding a secret childhood trauma. Either way, the dialogue in and of itself overwhelmed me. Just the thought of talking about what happened or that I might be in trouble put me into self-soothe mode. After all, it was supposed to be a fun weekend adventure with my girlfriend, but it was anything but fun; it was horrific. Besides, one day I would find my voice, find the courage, and find the nerve to let it all out. Some happened right away, some years later, and some reenacted again and again in my head, until the Lord wiped away those tears, those memories, and those traumas. He took it away. And what's more, He wants to heal us all.

Yet, before I open up, once more that latent drama inside my head turned me into a foodie, living to eat. Food was an unforeseen coping skill; regardless, it became pleasure personified. Weighing more in sixth grade than I do now resulted in the never-ending task of finding clothes to fit me, and it was a hard task to accomplish, especially when the mother-daughter duo turned shopping into a challenging chore to be lived through. And in spite of the shame of the childhood trauma, that wasn't the only thing I was about to feel shame for. It was finding clothes to fit me—not too tight, not too loose, but clothes that fit just right. Only I felt ashamed of my size and the way I looked. Finally, as Mom's last resort when it came to shopping with me, she would begrudgingly take me to the women's department to try on clothes—not to the children's department, mind you, but to the women's section of the department store. At first, I didn't know what she was up to, but once we were inside of the women's department, I got it. This, of course, led to my further embarrassment over buying clothes in a larger size to fit me.

One time, Mom was especially angry because she could not find anything to fit me. Then she became the angriest I had ever seen when I came out of the women's dressing room wearing a size 18. What that really meant was she would have to hem the Sunday dress in time for me to wear for Easter, which was right around the corner. The dress was way too long, as it was designed for a grown-up. That left her fuming and belittling me for gaining more weight. I already felt inadequate and miserable due to the secret I was carrying around, but the clothes shopping experience only added insult to injury. It was as if I had done something reprehensible, and we were just trying to find a dress to fit me in time for Easter. To make matters worse, husky sizes (and yes, that is what they called them back then) and half sizes were available in the preteen aisle (but only in limited amounts), and Mom was mad at me while we searched through the in-between sizes for something to fit. And nothing would fit. If those limited plus sizes weren't in stock, that is how we ended up looking in the adult section of the store. When that happened, I was mortified. Terror welled up inside me, knowing Mom wasn't done scolding me for being overweight.

Well, being in the adult section also meant, "Shame on you for getting like this," or so I was told and led to believe. Additionally, I would have never realized I was stuck inside a volatile, emotionally abusive relationship with my own mother—one that caused me in the future to run off to college, so I could get away from her screaming nonsense at me in the house. Most of the time for absolutely nothing, she would take her frustrations out on me. It was all unnecessary, as there are other, more positive and constructive ways to communicate effectively. In the future, healing would come, understanding would come, and forgiveness would spring out of me. Until then, publicly, I felt humiliated when I went shopping with my mother. I felt really bad, and I felt ugly, like the ugly duckling trapped in an awkward, shameful body. It felt like the entire world was watching me, and nobody liked what they saw.

Eventually, Mom stopped bringing me with her to shop for clothes as I got older (and certainly that was a good thing under the circumstances). Then I would come home from school to find whatever was there was there for me to wear—period. I don't know about you, but she never let me pick out my own stylish outfits when the sizes were available or allow me to choose my own clothes from a catalog. Try that one on for size. No, on second thought, let it go. Although, I must add, I sure made up for it in the future. Not only was I able to work as a personal stylist and wardrobe consultant during my college years, but later, I became a fashion-forward, bargain-hunting fashionista who loves a good sale.

Anyhow, besides the inner turmoil lingering inside my head, the combination of stressors guaranteed an outcome: emotional overeating as a tween. Of course, I wouldn't have known the meaning of that term back then, being that I was a child. Plus, the words had not yet been coined or explained. I couldn't verbalize why I turned into a foodie; it just became part of my young life. Still, I had not leaked out my traumatic experience occurring in the summer between fourth and fifth grades. No one knew, but it was compounded by being bullied inside and outside of school for my ever-increasing size and privately berated at home for gaining weight. There were too many reasons why I ate in seclusion. For instance, if nobody could see me eat, then no one could make fun of me. Food became the delicious part of life.

THE BURIED SECRET

Yet there was *one* secret I was afraid to open up about, and that secret plagued my thoughts. I reasoned over and over, "I'll get in trouble for this one for sure." How could I truly talk about it? I was told to be quiet until sixth grade, and additionally, our neighbor told me not to tell anyone. I knew something was wrong, but nobody talked about being molested, what it meant, what it entailed, or what the signs were to look for if you were in trouble. None of it was ever openly discussed. So how would I know? On top of that, while I was growing up, my mother frequently told me, "It's all in your head." That was her response to everything I shared, so I thought how I *felt* about what happened must also all be in my head. In other words, it didn't exist. That rhetoric and those words taught me to discredit my inner signals and ignore any warning signs that could be legit, and that got me into misfortune on numerous occasions. Never ignore your inner warning signs. They could be right, and they could save your life.

Instead, being told to be quiet and that it was all in my head," plus the bulling, was exacerbated by the childhood molestation. But the untold secret in itself compounded everything. It made me afraid to tell my mom, speak up, and share my awful secret. Besides, I didn't have my words. I felt that I was making it bigger than what it was, altogether discrediting the traumatic event. On the other hand, I felt terrible and guilty about hiding it too, like something was indeed (seriously) wrong, but I wasn't sure what to do, what to say, and how to stop the feelings—the pain. I had to tell someone what happened to me. Also, like I said, I was afraid of getting into trouble if I told anyone what happened on vacation with my best girlfriend's father, like it was my fault when it wasn't. "It never was your fault," I would one day (years later) be told. And, to top it off, I was repeatedly warned by my friend's father, "Don't tell your parents."

I didn't know (and how could I have known) that everything was intentionally done as a setup. It had all been contrived to hide the real truth, and that was part of the deception—being misled. To be misled, my girlfriend's father was about to set me up to not tell my parents, which is just one of the things he groomed me for, but I didn't know that was going on. The concept is called child grooming. Of course, my parents didn't know that something was going to happen to me, and I am guessing they'd never heard about that term either. But nowadays, you can watch a complete description of this definition on YouTube or read about it on Wikipedia. This free and immediate access to information on the web was certainly designed to educate parents and to protect children. That instant access to free knowledge wasn't readily available to either parent or child in the sixties. As you can see, we've come a long, long way.

What happened didn't feel right, but I *never* heard anyone discuss bad things happening to little girls in the home, in school, or on the news (although I didn't watch the news as a tween). I couldn't quite put it into words those awful feelings and my dreadful secret. I just knew that something was seriously wrong, and it consumed my private world.

MY CHILDHOOD SECRET EXPOSED

One of my best friends forever growing up was Amber. Of course, we never used the abbreviation BFF or term bestie. Yet she was one of my best girlfriends. Her family lived directly across the street from our house. When they moved in, I was one of the first to run over to meet her. Hence, she became my bestie on the block and one of the few chosen girlfriends I had in the neighborhood. We were considered girly girls, which meant we were not labeled tomboys, as that seemed to be a popular word back in the day. We were both rather shy and quiet, and we used to happily play back and forth between our two homes.

One of the things we enjoyed doing together at either house was listening to music. She liked country music, and I liked rock and roll. Back then, a single song could be on a seven-inch 45 rpm, or our parents would buy us a full-size vinyl 33 1/3 rpm record album containing our favorite hits to listen to. Today, our favorites are on an app on our phones. Outside of music, we enjoyed playing board games and paper dolls. I loved making paper dolls and owned a huge assortment of them. They were extremely popular and emulated most television series back in the sixties. Their popularity was comparable to the video games of today. The most enjoyable part was fitting the dolls in their own iconic wardrobes. Those retro styles included fashionable bell-bottoms, pop-art prints, and mod accessories, all of which can still be seen and worn today but arrayed our dolls in imaginary play.

One day Amber's father asked my father, "Can your daughter join us on a trip I am planning for Amber?" It was summertime, which was a perfect time for a vacation. At that point, Mr. Jones told my dad, "My wife and son are going out of town to visit her relatives, and Amber and I decided to do something fun for her birthday while they're gone, and she would like Grace to come." During their entire conversation, Amber and I were jumping up and down in the background, saying, "Please, please, pretty please!" Aside from our enthusiasm, my parents still needed time to consider his invitation; yet, in the end, they decided I could go.

Finally, the day arrived, and the three of us, Mr. Jones and two little girly girls, headed toward the mountains. Amber and I were beyond excited and kept asking the loaded question, "Are we there yet?" And his reply was always, "No, not yet." In the beginning, we were full of energy, but as time crept by, I was becoming restless with the long car ride.

As we were rambling down the road, Amber became sleepy and decided to take a nap on her half of the back seat in the car, while I sat on the other side peering out the window and watching the lovely scenery pass us by. It was while she was asleep that I recall her father saying to me, "It's very hot outside. Come and see how hot it is up front with the sun beating down on the windowpane."

Instantly, I felt awkward, and I tried to ignore his request in order to avoid getting close to him. I remember feeling quite uncomfortable and uneasy in the moment. Plus, I thought, *I don't want to obey him. It just doesn't feel right. I don't want to go up front.* Well, what would I know? I was told to obey him. At the time, those were just thoughts and feelings welling up inside me. But did my thoughts and feelings count or didn't they matter? Hesitating with those premonitions, I ended up ignoring myself. I had never been in such a predicament of uncertainty or under such circumstances and wasn't entirely sure what to say or do.

No sooner did those thoughts cross my mind, did Mr. Jones intervene in our conversation. Something terrible happened inside the car while Amber was sleeping. It must have been wrong because I suddenly felt overwhelmed and horrible all at the same time. With that, I froze up and instantly wanted to go home. *What do I do now?* I wondered. I looked at Amber, and she was still sleeping. Was she really sleeping? I was thinking, *I can't believe she's still sleeping. Would she just hurry up and wake up. If she wakes up, maybe he won't act like that anymore.* Panic set in, as I was beside myself and inconsolable. Now I was thinking, *The drive is taking forever. This isn't any fun. Where is home? I wish I were home. I wish I would have never come.*

After Amber woke up from her nap, her father assured us, "We're all going to have a great time together celebrating Amber's birthday." He quickly added, "Grace, you can call me Daddy while we're out of town instead of calling me Mr. Jones." I had been asked to call him Mr. Jones. While growing up, it was considered proper etiquette and part of being respectful to address an adult by his or her formal name. Today it's a debatable subject.

In regard to the new title being asked of me, when I heard Mr. Jones's comment, nothing would come out of my mouth concerning the new title. I just stared blankly at him in disbelief. *I'll never call you Daddy. I already have a Daddy*, I thought to myself. *All I want to do is go back home.* Yet here I was, stuck in some car and unable to leave—trapped. This led me to ask, "Are we there yet? Where are we anyway?" At that point, we were just about to cross state lines. It was different back then, but today the penalties are higher if you cross a border in order to molest a child.

TRYING TO SPEAK UP

Upon checking into the motel, Mr. Jones insisted that we change and get ready to go out for dinner. Supposedly, we were in some sort of rush, yet he wanted us all to take a shower after the long road trip. In my interpretation, I took that to mean we were each going to take a turn in the bathroom to shower and get ready. But that wasn't the case at all, and he had different intentions. Then all of a sudden, his objective became crystal clear when he firmly stated, "I want you both to do it this way. ... It will save us time." When I tried to say something and protest being in some chintzy motel bathroom together, he became instantly angry and authoritative. It was even worse when I nervously requested to be alone in order to avoid the togetherness that his request (really a demand) implied.

Right then, the little girl in me was trying to have a voice, trying to speak up to a parent, and trying to have a defense in the matter. She tried, but her voice was squelched. In return, Mr. Jones's voice became louder and his demeanor overbearing as he stood over me. Likewise, his tone and posture became threatening, as he bullied me into submitting to his demands. As I stared back at him and looked over at Amber, his deliberate directives got the best of me at the tender age of nine. Honestly, I was no match for him. Instead, I felt claustrophobic and once again trapped. I was now more afraid and unsure than ever before, but I obeyed the adult in front of me.

As I stood frozen in time, alarms went off inside my head saying, *What am I going to do? My parents said, "You can go, but listen to Mr. Jones. He's in charge." They told him he was in charge. Maybe I'm making something out of nothing. Maybe my feelings are wrong. Is he right? He can't be right. Maybe it's all in my head? But I've been told to listen to him and be polite. Plus, obey what my parents or he tells me to do or else. … But still, this feels wrong, not right.* Those statements had been drilled into my head along with hearing, "The world is filled with good people." That was my initial worldview, which just fell apart. My worldview was ideal, not real, and I was about to find out how real, not ideal, it would become.

Amber's father looked gigantic to me as a child, and his personality would switch on a dime, becoming altogether mean, like the story of Dr. Jekyll and Mr. Hyde. With his split personality, fear loomed over me when Mr. Hyde was present. That's when I was overcome with worry and concern, mistrust and dread. My deepest apprehension (knowing that I was in some sort of jeopardy) became reality when something shocking and appalling happened inside the stuffy little bathroom. I desperately wanted to be right with my intuition, just as much as I desperately wanted out of the room. I was more than claustrophobic. I was suffocating. My thoughts paralyzed me, as my voice was silenced once more when I tried to stand up for myself.

I could not have put it together right then that bad things can happen to good girls, but they did. None of it was my fault, absolutely none of it, and that was explained to me years later (many years later). It's not that I wanted such a long wait or that I wanted to carry a burden around inside my head, but that is exactly what happened until I became older. Moreover, breakthrough did come (because of Christ), along with freedom from the memories of the past. Christ came to set us all free—not just me.

Somehow, that minivacation ended up being nothing like I had anticipated or could have ever imagined. It was unlike anything I had ever experienced up until then—totally unrelatable. The overall excitement that Amber and I once had when we left, for me, had long vanished inside the car ride, and the exhilaration of the moment never did return. Everything had gone from bad to worse, and it was only day one. Most of all, I knew

I wasn't loving life right then. I never asked for that experience, and it was largely out of my control. Plus, I was stuck in another state, far away from everyone near and dear and far away from home.

None of that subject matter was ever portrayed on television at the time it took place in my life. And the weekend wasn't over; it had only just begun. To my knowledge, nothing existed on any channel referencing the molestation of a minor. Even if it were on television, I wouldn't have been permitted to watch it. You certainly can't say that today. Now, these subjects and public awareness of them have grown throughout the years, and it's being broadcast everywhere on the media today. I can only wish that I had been educated about this subject while growing up, but I'm glad it's being discussed today and for future generations. Back then, our family usually watched *The Brady Bunch, Get Smart,* and *The Partridge Family,* to name a few shows, and they would never have touched a topic such as this.

In my innocent mind, those shows (that I loved to watch) represented a perfect world to live in until I felt ruined by life. The shows contained no real drama to help in my time of need, for someone in desperate need of answers and help on hard-to-talk-about subject matter. Had I seen it, had I heard about it, I would have said something. Instead, I repressed the pain. In my small world, not only did I look forward to watching those shows, but I still enjoyed collecting and playing with dolls, especially paper dolls, like I had mentioned earlier, and Barbies. It was a child's world full of innocence, make-believe, and play. I really didn't know anything different up until I was molested. Then feelings I never wanted or asked for surfaced yet remained hidden. The crime against my innocence left me feeling filthy, broken, and stifled.

On top of the loss of innocence, every single week my family would wear our Sunday best and attend church. That meant my sister and I would reshine our black or white (given the season), patent leather shoes for Sunday school, put on one of our three dresses that we each owned, and then head off to church. Our Sunday services included Sunday school, worship, and a sermon, concluding with an altar call and prayer. Although tough subjects were not tackled from the pulpit, such as this chapter, today this subject and more are being addressed on various Christian platforms. These platforms have opened the door for healing and help to be made available everywhere you turn, touch a button, or attend church. Thank

God for open doors that no man can shut so that healing and restoration can take place in people's lives.

Yet, until there was change, I needed more preparation to be out in the world, and it wasn't available. Today you can surf the web for answers. Additionally, everything has changed legally since the sixties. Now there is Erin's Law, which covers nearly all fifty states. This campaign exists in the schools to teach children and their families about the prevention of childhood sexual abuse by predators. Back in the day, nothing existed to prepare and protect children. As a result, behavior I never heard exists in the world, such as being molested by a pedophile, existed in my tiny world, yet it was unspoken. Looking back now, knowing God protected me then, it could have been fatal. That traumatic event was the loss of my innocence. Being in that situation, I was too young to know our actual whereabouts except that I knew we were in a different state. I also didn't know how to handle myself in such a crisis; it simply had never been explained to me. How could I have dreamt something like that existed? Besides, I was powerless to protect myself in that instance and isolated from everyone except Amber. How could I put together that I was intentionally being drawn away as prey? It was supposed to be a birthday party for two excited tweens. But then, more than ever, the dream was to go home. Right then, there was no place like home.

When I look back over my life, I've discovered what remains through it all is the beauty of knowing Christ. He brought me out of the pain, the trauma, and the childhood memory of something largely out of my control. On a personal note, He didn't just come to set me free. If this has happened to you, there is a way out of your distress. Psalms 118:5 reads, "I called on the Lord in distress; The Lord answered me and set me in a broad place." This means when you call upon the Lord—now, not later— He will answer you in your heart of hearts, right where it hurts the most, more than others may even know. He came to set you free from what has you all tied up on the inside. Possibly, your brokenness is hidden from others, and you've learned to conceal it, but not from the Lord. He came to mend your broken heart so that you can go forward into everything He has planned for you. Just pray, just ask, and be encouraged by this verse as well: "I would have lost heart, unless I had believed that I would see the goodness of the Lord in the land of the living. Wait on the Lord; be of good courage, and He shall strengthen your heart; wait, I say, on the Lord" (Ps. 27:13–14). This verse is what the Lord wants to do in your heart and mine when we turn to Him.

Of course, in working through the trauma, there were times when I racked my brain on what I could have done differently. One such thought was about the prehistoric phone system. Seriously, there was no phone inside the motel room. Talk about primitive. … But I do remember one hanging outside when we walked by. It was a dial-up, or rotary, pay phone. Amber and I couldn't leave the room to go outside. We weren't allowed or we would be in trouble. In the past, it was complicated to call home from state to state if there were no telephone operators available to speak with. You needed change plus additional change to add to stay on the phone, and I had none. Regardless, I couldn't reach the pay phone outside even if I wanted to. I wasn't that tall. Afterward, I used to dream of that phone, wishing I could have used it. There was no 911; it hadn't even been created. There were *no* cell phones, texting, or tracking systems; they were nonexistent.

All of the above is just an afterthought compared to the compliant little girl who obeyed adults and stayed inside that musty little motel room. I wish I could have solved the problem back in the sixties. I wish I had known what to do when you feel uncomfortable. … I wish I could have known what a predator looked like, acted like, or sounded like. But how would I know? I never heard the word *pedophile*, and that is because no one ever used that word. I didn't hear of a sexual predator preying on children until years later. That you should run if you can, but I didn't know that either, and the instinct to run never occurred to me because I was busy obeying what I was told to do. On top of being afraid, it was not a safe environment with my girlfriend, as I was first led to believe; rather, I was just trying to survive a nightmare. I wished I could have saved her, helped her, the little girl in me, but I couldn't—not yet. But in the future, I absolutely could.

THE DREADED NIGHT

After our fast-food dinner, the three of us returned to the motel. That's when Mr. Jones told us to quickly get ready for bed, but it seemed too early for bed. Amber's father was going to step out for a bit once we were in bed. Most likely, that is why he rushed us off to bed. Oddly, in that strange, foreign place we had no babysitter. Without a doubt, at home I would have had a sitter, especially at night. Only here, he was going to leave us alone in the evening, and we were in another state. How far from home? Hours and hours—a day's drive. We were in a remote motel in an obscure town somewhere in the mountains, unexpectedly, we were going to be left alone. He also told us, "You're old enough to stay in the room by yourselves." That is not true if you look it up online even today, but that is what we were told. We had a two-bedroom motel room, and Mr. Jones stayed in a room by himself with a Jack-and-Jill bathroom in-between his room and ours. Amber and I had two double beds on our side, one for each one of us. Once he made sure we were tucked in for the night, Mr. Jones stepped out after warning us not to open the door or go outside for any reason whatsoever.

Upon leaving, dusk turned into twilight, and I couldn't fall asleep. No wonder sleep escaped me. I was afraid of Mr. Jones leaving us alone and his imminent return. Plus, I was in a worn-out, rundown, dark, and dreary room located in an unrecognizable town, and even though Amber was with me, I felt trapped. I missed my own bedroom with the smell of fresh, scented sheets and my own clean pillow where I could pull the covers up around me and feel safe. However, new thoughts began to plague my mind, *What if. . . .* That meant I began to think of the worst-case scenarios. To stop the what-ifs, I crawled in bed with Amber. Originally, it was supposed to be a tiny slumber party. Both she and I had our very own room together. Maybe a pillow fight and jumping from bed to bed, giggles and all, but none of that happened. And obviously it was no slumber party.

To top off the night, and much to my amazement, the half of her bed that I wanted to sleep in was wet. *Wet with urine, or did someone spill a glass of water on the bed? Did Amber do that?* I wondered, but I didn't ask. I can't believe I didn't ask what happened. All I know was that her eyes were closed, and perhaps she had already fallen asleep. Maybe the owners of the hotel didn't make the bed fresh and clean like mine at home. Maybe that's all it was. But, nonetheless, her open side of the bed was wet enough that I couldn't sleep there.

I cringed with the thought of the wet bet and panicked too due to the fact that I didn't feel good about the night. That was the real reason I wanted to sleep in her double bed in the first place—no girly girl stuff that night. Truthfully, I was more afraid to stay in the bed next to her alone because I was extremely worried that Mr. Jones would intrude upon my space when he returned. He already had intruded upon my space. Regardless, that gave credence to my what-if thoughts as they continued to haunt me. I couldn't seem to get them out of my head. I'm not entirely sure why I continued to think like that. A premonition perhaps? Yet those were the thoughts running through my brain, not sleep but, *What-if.* ...

Even though I was small and quite young, I couldn't escape my feelings or thoughts that night. I lay awake fighting a sense of gloom and doom in the air. Was it real or imaginary? Or was that in some small way a warning? Were my instincts taking over? Was I wrong, or was I right after all? I just knew that something wasn't right with the night. Something wasn't right at all. I questioned, *What is wrong with this night?* I couldn't quite put my finger on it, and I couldn't define it or figure it out. Feelings of anxiety surrounded my night, and my thoughts became an unsolved mystery.

Still, Mr. Jones had not arrived. As I lay in the dry bed right next to Amber, I could hardly fall asleep. Again, sleep eluded me. Of course, Amber could fall sleep. I couldn't believe she could sleep, but there she was, sleeping away the night. Was she faking it? She had to have heard me tossing and turning, but she lay motionless. Anyhow, that really didn't matter at all right then. Yet there I lay awake, dreading the night. I continued thinking, *Maybe I'm overreacting and it's all in my head—not real, not happening.* Anyhow, the little girl in me really hoped to be wrong.

The hours slowly crept by, and I never did fall into any kind of deep sleep. Then Mr. Jones returned. All of a sudden, I could hear the door to our room open. Instantly (and instinctively), it became my turn to pretend to be asleep and lay motionless. I dare not move. My heart was pounding so hard and so fast that I could hear it, but I dare not move. Immediately, I began to think, *Maybe I'm jumping to conclusions. Possibly he's just checking on us to see that we're OK. Maybe this is just a bad dream.* But it wasn't.

That's when Mr. Jones came into our room, not to wake Amber up, but me. I was the one in jeopardy again. In my fake slumber, my only shred of hope was that he would turn around and leave once he saw us both sleeping, yet that didn't work like I had hoped. My fake sleep didn't work either, and sure enough, he began to shake me, proceeding to wake me up. He leaned over and whispered into my ear, "Come with me. I want to tell you the surprise I have planned for Amber's birthday."

Right away, I hoped Amber would wake up. She didn't. Was she pretending? Was she still pretending even after I tried to make some noise? Surreal. She didn't move a muscle. Then Mr. Jones told me, "Don't wake her up. This is supposed to be our little secret."

I felt instantly overwhelmed (again) and caught in some kind of trap as I was dragged away against my will into another room. I tried to protest, but it went unheard. Rather, my protest was deliberately ignored. I tried to tell him, "I want to sleep. Let me get some sleep. I'm tired." But that too was ignored. I was breaking up inside, which left me fully traumatized and wide awake. On top of that, he smelled like liquor, as he must have been drinking. He wasn't making any rational sense because he was inebriated, and I had never been around a drunk in my entire young life. But that was beside the point, and I was beyond startled. That was when some unpredictable, unimaginable, unprecedented circumstance happened to me—a child. I couldn't save the child right then. I couldn't spare the child the trauma she would endure, which is more than I should say right now and, for the most part, is better left unsaid. But you can only imagine how broken and fragmented I soon became.

In that tragic moment, I know now, although I didn't know then—I wasn't alone in my horrendous, most difficult moment. The Lord was in the room with me. If you have been through a tragedy, know you were never alone. He promises to never leave us or forsake us. (See Deuteronomy 31:8.) The Bible also declares in Psalms 23:4, "Yea, though I walk through the valley of the shadow of death, I will fear no evil; for You are with me; Your rod and Your staff, they comfort me."

At the time, my only thought became, *I have to get out of this room and get back to Amber. If I can get to Amber, I'll be safe.* I kept repeating out loud, "I'm so tired. I'm sleepy. I've got to get some sleep." My main goal was Amber. I felt if I could get to her, there would be two of us, and

I might be safe. Two are better than one. When I managed to get away, I quickly ran to Amber's bed. I dove right into her bed on the side that was wet, not caring in the least that it was wet. And she still refused to wake up. All the while, I lay there quietly trembling, huddled in a fetal position next to her and holding my breath. I lay quiet, not moving a muscle, not moving an inch. My thoughts rambled to, *What if Mr. Jones returns?* More than ever, I just wanted to be home in my own dry, sweet-smelling bed.

When morning came, Amber was excited; it was her special day. She ran into her father's room and hopped into bed with him under the covers. The sun was shining, and rays from the sun entered the room. Reluctantly, I entered Mr. Jones's room too and stood at the foot of the bed, silent and sleepy. Amber and her father begged me to climb into bed with them in order to snuggle under the covers together and watch cartoons. Determined, I held my ground saying, "No. I'll just sit at the corner of the bed and watch TV."

I felt the sun, and I could see the sunshine, but I felt dead inside. I wanted to scream and did not, I wanted to go home and could not, and I wanted to cry and did not. Amber, the birthday girl, was happy, and I was definitely miserable, pretending it was a great day when it was anything but that. Her father kept saying privately and in front of his daughter, "Call me Daddy. C'mon, I'll be your dad while you're away from home." Amber, likewise, urged me to call him daddy. He wasn't my dad, I wasn't his daughter, and I wasn't about to play their game. Moreover, the big surprise for Amber was visiting a horse farm and going horseback riding. I was numb, but I should have been ecstatic because I truly love horses. Instead, I was void of any happy feelings on her special day, while she appeared happy and excited.

FINALLY, I'M HOME

Upon arriving home, I could barely contain myself as I ran inside to hug my mom. Tears began streaming down my face, altogether startling her. Immediately, concern spread across her face as she asked, "Is everything all right?" She appeared to be looking deep inside of me for the correct answer.

I replied, "Yes, everything's OK."

She kept asking the same question over and over, insisting on a different answer. But then she interjected, "Why are you crying?"

I stammered, "I'm crying because I'm so glad to be home. I think I'm just homesick. That's all." The trauma of the molestation remained repressed inside me and, to a greater degree, stuck inside my head. I was afraid to talk about it. Was it the fear of Mr. Jones because he told me not to tell? Was it the fear of my mother getting mad at me? Was it the fear that I did something wrong? Was it the worry and fear that I would get into trouble if I told? I believe it was all of those things. Because of that, I hid my nonexistent words and my feelings, and I stuffed them down inside of me, afraid to share. I needed to find my words and get over the fear (for whatever reason) in order to explain what Mr. Jones said and did to me.

DEFENDING CHILDREN

Time ticked by. I'm not sure if it was six months or a year and six months, but finally, one night I couldn't keep my dreadful secret any longer and told my mother. Once my father knew, he consulted an attorney. What I do know today is that my parents tried to help with the limited resources that were available in the sixties. By 1967, most states had child protection laws in place, but they were still in their infancy and underdeveloped from state to state. Absolutely no education existed on any level from the schools on through the medical profession. By 1974, a governmental leadership role was established with the passage of the Child Abuse Prevention and Treatment Act of 1974 (CAPTA), but it was way too late for me. Time had already passed me by.

In the meantime, my parents' attorney needed additional information regarding Mr. Jones. During their fact-gathering mission, I needed to ask Amber questions regarding her father without letting her know it wasn't a game we were going to play. It was more like an undercover mission. They needed personal details in order to press charges or to find any prior records. So she and I played a word-guessing game, charades, to retrieve the answers. They needed his birth date. That was one of the questions I had to ask. Once I had the data, it was then forwarded to the attorney. Later I was told too much time had passed and nothing could be done legally. Or was it a matter of money at the time? There is no way I could have known those details at that tender age, as our family didn't openly discuss finances back then. Either way, I was not included in any of the conversations between my parents and the attorney. Yet that was the explanation given to me—that too much time had lapsed. Unfortunately, those events took place before the statute of limitations had changed, which allowed for more time to press charges. I discovered that decades later while doing some research on the internet for this book.

Furthermore, my parents didn't believe in therapy, and the church they attended didn't support counseling either—both sad and true. Even so, I recently heard on a Christian broadcasting network that, in some circles today, there are still churches that do not embrace counseling or therapy. In regard to our family, not only did I not get to see anyone to discuss what occurred, but we didn't talk about what happened after those initial days. The subject completely disappeared as if nothing ever took place. It was erased; except for in my head, the memories were stuck inside. Certainly, dealing with the repercussions was harder for me than for them. I sure thought about it in the years that followed because the nightmare still existed in my head. I had to wait for the right time to present itself for me to get it out of my head, and the Lord opened up a door of opportunity in the future. "I waited patiently for the Lord; and He inclined to me, and heard my cry" (Ps. 40:1). And so, one day the Lord showed me a way out of the trauma.

However, the vivid memory (prior to the inner healing) followed me like a silent killer. It wasn't until I became an adult that I finally began to deal with what happened to me inside of Christian counseling and within a church that supported inner healing. Indeed, times have changed.

My healing journey began at a church conference for women who have been sexually abused. Finally, the subject matter wasn't hidden any longer, and scores of hurting women were in attendance from all over. I was surprised when I saw hundreds of women in attendance, so many that it was hard to find a parking spot when I first arrived. They came in hurting *but left as miracles.* My parents might not have believed in therapy back then, but I did later, and I reaped the benefits from seeing a godly therapist and by attending the above conference. It was comforting to know that I wasn't alone during those events. Again, the Lord was by my side throughout the entire process.

Without a doubt, I was transformed. The result: He healed me by taking away the pain of the traumatic memory, and I know the Lord uses people at times to assist in the process of healing, as He did in that situation. It wasn't an instant healing (as I would have liked) but a gradual inner healing that took place over time. For both, whether healing takes place instantaneously (because I know this happens) or gradually, immersing yourself in reading the Bible is one of the keys to overcoming adversity. In Romans 12:2, it says, "And do not be conformed to this world, but be transformed by the renewing of your mind, that you may prove what is that good and acceptable and perfect will of God." Plus, in Philippians 4:8, it reads, "Finally, brethren, whatever things are true, whatever things are noble, whatever things are just, whatever things are pure, whatever things are lovely, whatever things are of good report, if there is any virtue and if there is anything praiseworthy—meditate on these things." All being said, those life choices brought restoration.

It is never too late for healing and restoration to take place. So let's seize the day for a better tomorrow.

After those initial days as a child, my dad visited Amber's mother and told her the facts of the perpetration. Even though nothing could be done legally, my dad wasn't finished addressing the ongoing dilemma in my defense. At that point, Mrs. Jones went on to tell my dad, "This isn't new news. He's done this before." That was actually terrible news to hear. Besides, after the molestation, I was afraid to play at Amber's house because I was afraid to see her father. But after the parental discussion, I wasn't allowed to play at her house ever again. Amber was only permitted to play at our house. Not too soon after the confrontation, the family moved out of state, and the parents divorced. After they left, I never heard from Amber again. As a teenager, the biggest news I heard years later was that Mr. Jones had gone to prison. As a predator and as a serial pedophile, he sexually molested again. With the changing laws, he was finally caught and prosecuted, hopefully to the fullest extent of the law. I'm saying that for all the children he violated and should be accountable for. Today he is no longer living, and I have long since forgiven him.

Back in the sixties, special license plates issued for pedophiles in order to protect children didn't exist. Additionally, they did not have to register as a child sex offender, forewarning an entire neighborhood. There was also no App Store where you could download helpful crime maps, unlike today. Without that sort of intel, all I know is that there were other victims before me, but were there others on our street? I'll never know because the laws to protect children didn't exist like they do now. We didn't talk about it as a community or nationally like we do today. Until then, Mr. Jones was free to live on our street filled with children, and I was molested by this criminal pedophile. At the time I lost my innocence as a child, I was an A student and on the honor roll at school, and unbelievably, I enjoyed writing book reports and reading books. In other words, I was a real bookworm. At home, I liked to watch *Mayberry, Lassie,* and *Lost in Space,* and I still loved playing with dolls, along with earning awards and patches as a Girl Scout.

When I look back, it's hard to know that I couldn't save her—the little girl in me. Only God could. I couldn't spare her the trauma, but there is a God who heals trauma of all sorts. I'm grateful to the Lord that I walked away in the end after Mr. Jones took me to another state. When I look back today, I realize it could have ended tragically. And I've always wondered about Amber. Was she okay? I'll never know. I have often wondered if she was pretending to be asleep in the bedroom when her father woke me up. I'll never know the truth. Certainly, I couldn't verbalize at the age of nine what I can articulate today. What is tragic? That no one ever mentioned a topic such as this openly, which I can freely write about today. Also, because of a lack of resources, I carried it around in my head and never shared my awful secret. For years, in wasn't addressed. There were no social media outlets to inform or to share or to tell someone or even to compare notes online. Today, there are plenty of resources and platforms available, and children are better prepared to act, not react, if a crisis like this should arise. Thankfully, it's a new era, and things have changed—in some ways for the better.

IN CONCLUSION
INNER HEALING AND RESTORATION

In Romans 2:11, it reads, "For there is no partiality with God." What He can do for one, He will do for another. The Lord healed the inside of me, truly setting me free from the past. "Who the Son sets free, is free indeed" (John 8:36). Likewise, He can heal and set you free from your childhood memories. Claim these scriptures for yourself. He freed me from the trauma and fears of my youth, and He will do the same for you. Whether it was a heavy-handed authority figure, someone who has molested you, or childhood bullies, all of those memories can be healed. Out of everything that happened in my life, and possibly your life too, this scripture in Genesis 50:20 says, "But as for you, you meant evil against me; but God meant it for good, in order to bring it about as it is this day, to save many people alive." You may never know how going through adverse and life-altering circumstances can be turned around and used to help others. Allow God to take what the enemy meant for evil and turn it around for good. His plan is to give us beauty for ashes, thereby making life sweet again. (See Isaiah 61:3.)

Forgiveness is another key to healing and restoration. Don't forget to check out the Keys to Forgiveness Scale in the appendix, and also take a look at the "Strategies for Overcoming" section. Here, you will find useful tips to help you let go and overcome any memories or trauma from the past.

CHAPTER 5

THE MEAN GIRLS IN SCHOOL (MOB BULLYING)

> Don't speak poorly of others. You don't need to minimize
> other people to maximize your own potential.
> — Brendon Burchard

Before junior high began, my preference to handle my hidden stressors
was to become a foodie. Only I turned being a foodie into an addiction,
and that addiction came naturally to me. In looking back at those prior
childhood events that emotionally traumatized me, it boiled down to
more than just bioengineered, sugar-laden foods; it was rather the muzzle
placed over my mouth for what I could and couldn't say while growing
up. So food turned into a coping mechanism while I was young. Eating
was pleasurable, and the food tasted and smelled great, except for, of
course, tuna noodle casserole, liver and onions, and canned peas or lima
beans. My preference was my grandmother's homemade ice cream and
Breyers Neapolitan ice cream. Those yummy dairy desserts not only felt
good going down but tasted even better smothered in thick hot fudge,
whipping cream, and salted pecans. Sweets were an enjoyable bright spot
in my life, turning me into a reactive food addict. What I could control as
a child was my self-soothing food addiction. I ate myself silly (sometimes
in secret) to cope with the sexual molestation and bullying done privately
and publicly until my dear grandmother intervened one summer, thereby
changing my life.

Not only did I spend most of my childhood and teen years consuming
a diet rich in sugar; I paid a price for doing so. Amazingly, I must have

thought sugar was an entire food group on the food pyramid while growing up. Sugar promotes tooth decay, and subsequently, most of my teeth are either filled or capped. I know that sounds gross, but it's true. As a teenager, I recall my mom urging me to visit the dentist before my father's dental insurance ran out on me. (Due to my age and their divorce, monies would soon stop.) Then, upon sitting in the dentist chair, he said, "You have eighteen cavities that need filled!" Well, that's a lot of amalgam fillings, to say the least. So in hearing that startling news, I about fell off the chair—for real.

RIGHT BEFORE THE MEAN GIRLS

Let me back up a bit to the summer I stayed with my grandmother, and she literally did a food intervention, saving my life. She staged it before the term, strategy, or plan was ever devised. When my grandma intervened, she told me, "I'm going to help you lose weight." That's when she showed me how to choose healthy foods and to eat this and not that, and I dropped the pounds. Plus, she challenged me. She offered to pay me for every pound I lost (cha-ching). Grandma wasn't sure how much to pay me, and I'm sure you'll get a chuckle out of this today. She wasn't sure if it should be twenty-five cents per pound or a dollar a pound. In time, she said, "I'm so glad I only paid you twenty-five cents a pound, or I'd go broke!" I know you're thinking that payout is both humorous and maybe cheap compared to today, but it wasn't back in the day.

The absolute best part of Grandma's program was that I started losing weight right away. Some of the foods that she cut out immediately were all condiments (mayo, ketchup, dressings, syrup, etc.), and no butter or sour cream on my baked potato. No desserts. No candy. No pop. No fried food, fast food, or boxed food. Instead, it was baked, steamed, or broiled, and I could have all the veggies I could eat. The funny thing is, I'm still like this today for the most part. Grandma also changed the Wonder Bread to wheat bread, changed dry cereals to cooked oats or Cream of Wheat, and cut out the Pop-Tarts, donuts, and pancakes with syrup. Instead of hot dogs and lunch meat, she prepared lean cuts of meat.

Furthermore, Grandma changed my portion size, which didn't include second or third or fourth helpings like I was accustomed to sneaking in. By the way, did you know the size of plates used today have changed, becoming altogether larger? In the end, all of Grandma's changes in my diet worked, and the other best part was paying me to lose the weight. What an incentive! It was an effective reward system she utilized. Certainly, that small price per pound wouldn't work today. However, Grandma taught me what to eat and what not to eat. By the end of my summer, we went shopping, and I proudly picked out a pair of blue, suede shoes and a purse to match for a job well done. By the time fall hit, I entered seventh grade a whole new person and a whole new size, and I was happy with me. That marked the beginning of my weight-loss transformation.

To top it off, credit goes to my grandma for not only changing my life but changing my diet and teaching me about real food. She left me armed with the knowledge that manufactured or processed foods, along with eating fast food, helped me to become chronically overweight and sick. But I wouldn't have known that as a child until she took the time to explain it to me. My grandmother worked as a kitchen manager in an elementary school, overseeing the kitchen staff and the students' diet, making changes for everyone where and when she could. For years, french fries and pop were not allowed on the menu; now they are. Simply put, her menu plan changed my future.

After my weight loss, Grandma confided, "I thought if I didn't step in, the kids would continue to poke fun at you, and I wanted to put an end to it (the bullying), before you entered high school."

That defining moment impacted me forever. I'm grateful for the many ways she demonstrated her love. To me, my dear grandmother was a positive role model, a mentor, and like a mother to me. For her time and love, I feel extremely thankful and grateful. We all need people like that in our lives to help grow us. And if we don't have people like that in our lives, we need to seek out and find positive mentors.

Now to bring you up to speed, just before I entered middle school, the community built a brand-new school, and I was more than eager to not only see it but to attend. Every suburban elementary school in the area planned to send their seventh and eighth graders to one main school district. It was a huge school, and if you can imagine hundreds of seventh and eighth graders all going through puberty at the same time, bussed in, and placed under one roof, then you can imagine a lot of hormones raging. My grandmother must have known that beforehand when she set out to change my size. Her food intervention was a lifesaver both psychologically and physically. She spared me from being bullied in middle school, or so I thought. In my defense, she often said, "I can't bear the thought of you entering these high school years being chubby, knowing the teenagers will probably harass you some more." Up until then, fat-shaming was all I knew—not from her but from others. Furthermore, that term remained unaddressed in society back then until the advent of the internet frenzy. Regardless, I was ready for a new me, and I'm so glad I stayed the summer with my grandma. No regrets here.

When seventh grade began, the kids barely recognized me because my appearance had changed. I was unprepared for that surprise. It was all good, of course. The students instantly stopped bullying me for being overweight, just like Grandma had said. Not only that, but I am sure my mom was way too happy to buy new clothes for me, unlike before. For certain, last year's clothes wouldn't fit, and a new wardrobe was in order. That left me more than thrilled due to so many positive changes. Not only was I attending a new school wearing new clothes, but there was also a brand-new me.

By the time eighth grade rolled around, I had taken off the rest of the excess weight. It was also the summer of my first true love. His name was Brad. I hardly ate that summer because I was so excited to be with him. I used to ride my bike back and forth to his house just to see him. I'm guessing the round trip was somewhere around ten miles, give or take. So between my new diet and having a steady boyfriend, along with the continued aerobics, I lost the extra pounds, thereby tightening and firming my teenage silhouette. Out of that came more good news: I had to get another new wardrobe for school. Of course, that didn't bother me one bit. Who wouldn't mind more new clothes in a different size? What an exciting reward for losing all the weight! Only that time I reached between a size 7 and 8 in the youth department! Gone were the husky-sized clothes. And just to think, once upon a time I wore a size 18 in the women's department. Overall, that was a huge achievement and an amazing transformation. Then, to top it off, I decided to let my hair grow long and color it blonde by the end of summer. That led to one final reward: Brad. He liked the new me too.

So, when eighth grade began, I was more than excited and filled with anticipation of what another new year might bring. Again, nobody knew me, and I was back at the same school as the year before. Unbelievably, they didn't recognize me at all. Change was for the best, and I even decided to try out for cheerleading at the beginning of the school year. Although I had the courage to give cheerleading a try, I had not practiced enough to qualify to win. Still, I was glad that I gave it a shot. Prior to that experience, I would have been disqualified as a contender purely based on size. And, yes, they really did do that back then. Thankfully, times have changed, and the rules have improved for those involved. Anyhow, I remained hopeful and optimistic at the beginning of the school year.

A NEW ME REJECTED

Everything was great until my first love dropped me. Like a hot potato, he dropped me. Brad was now attending a junior high school located in another city, while I remained in middle school. It felt like we were worlds apart. That's when he crushed both my ego and my heart. I pinned his decision on Josh, Brad's friend, because Josh informed him, "Grace is getting too much attention from the other guys here at school." That kind of attention was entirely foreign to me, sporting a new figure, a new hair color and style, and, well, a totally new me. That kind of special attention was not only a new experience for me, but it felt good in a great sort of way. Rather, it was lacking in my younger years. It had been altogether different from when I was heavy; some of the guys would call me every fat-shaming name you could think of. What a complete turnaround for my ears to hear. Whatever else was being said between Josh and Brad I wasn't privy to, but after Josh spoke, that was the end of our summer romance once school was back in session. Was the breakup because of Josh, was it the distance between us, or was it me? I'll never know, but I'm sure I wasn't the only person who lost her first true love in high school, although it sure felt that way. The loss left my head spinning and stirred up emotions I didn't want (again). That breakup completely shattered my thinking. *There will never be another Brad, like my first true love,* I thought. Of course, who knows all about true love in eighth grade?

Besides, why did those two guys continue to find fault with me simply for saying hi to the new guys in school? That was what the conflict was all about. Josh had seen me greeting the new students, learning their names, and talking to them too inside of school. That was all that was ever said or done. Nothing more. Where did that unforeseeable rule come from anyhow? Where guys could talk to girls, but girls could not talk to guys or they would be in trouble? Experiencing my first breakup was painful and rough enough, to say the least. And it was Josh who delivered the news to me, not Brad. (Today I know some people text to break up. Imagine that.) Yet all I knew was that I had done nothing wrong. Maybe Brad was controlling. Maybe he was insecure, or quite possibly he just wasn't into me. Or perhaps it was Josh's fault altogether by judging and gossiping about me. I'll never know the truth, but they were both wrong, if you ask me. I couldn't believe I couldn't say hi to a guy. What's up with that? Especially when I was finding my voice.

That crazy, sudden rejection from Brad sent me on a search. I wasn't completely intentional about finding someone, but it led me to unconsciously begin looking for a replacement boyfriend so that I could quickly get over Brad. But that idea didn't work for me. No matter which guy I started to like or who started to like me, the relationship always seemed to end after a week or two of being together. Most of our going together, as it was called in the seventies, consisted of holding hands (if that) or walking down the hallway to our next class—no dating or kissing. And, for the most part, I'm speaking for myself on that interpretation of the term *going together* because I know there are other definitions out there. Still, I couldn't find anyone to replace Brad the entire school year. Instead, I had guys as friends and no boyfriend for a while.

Incidentally, after school was out for the summer, Brad and I did get back together. I was beyond excited with our reunion, so much so that I introduced him to my very best girlfriend, my BFF. Mobile texting has created short (convenient) abbreviations, but the term *BFF* didn't exist back then. My BFF wouldn't be my best friend forever—how sad.

Anyhow, after we got back together, my BFF and Brad began secretly dating behind my back. Now, that outcome of the two of them together would have never entered my mind, and that caught me sideways. The whole thing, the whole setup, on top of the betrayal, wrecked me. I could have never dreamt that introducing them to one another would backfire. Their relationship quickly dissolved my friendship with my best friend—both of them, actually. Four years later, they married! Imagine that. As you may have guessed, their dating didn't go over well with me when I saw them at school or on the bus holding hands or kissing. It took a while to shrug off and let go of it all, but I really did get over Brad for good and moved on.

CLIQUES AND GROUPS

While we're on the subject of high school, it seems appropriate to mention that adolescence seems to add social cliques to life, regardless of whether you belong to one. Our school was no different. Our cliques ran under various nicknames. If you belonged to one of those groups and hung out with those particular teens, you were labeled as such. It became the group you identified with in and out of school. It was perceived as part of your identity. But I must interject here that your identity is not in what other people say about you, the labels they place upon you, or even what they say about you on any social media outlet. Overall, your true, authentic identity is in knowing Christ and His attributes and having a relationship with Him. I needed healing from being labeled, and maybe you need healing from being labeled. That's why I added this: It's never too late to pray and ask to be healed and restored. "Be anxious for nothing but in everything by prayer and supplication, with thanksgiving, let your requests be made known to God; and the peace of God, which surpasses all understanding, will guard your hearts and minds though Christ Jesus" (Phil. 4:6–7).

However, in the high school I attended, you would hear about the jocks (the athletic type), the troublemakers (the rebellious type), and the nerds (the bookworm type). Where those labels originated, I'll never know, but you'll find labels of some sort in just about every school system. It doesn't make a label right, but nonetheless, they existed then and now. I'm not sure if my parents even knew about those labels. They had their own nicknames for cliques in school, but we never talked about any labels whatsoever back then. I didn't volunteer which group I identified with given the stigma attached. I also wasn't in the right group at times because I tried several groups in order to find a fit. And, believe me, I know I wasn't the only one trying to fit in with so many new students.

During school, it appeared that everyone was busy trying to find themselves and where they fit inside a network of classmates, which were bussed in from all over town. It really became a time of self-discovery and camaraderie, alongside the age of self-development. Some of it was fun; some was *not*. Realistically, it depended on the choices one made. The outcome, hopefully, was to create a sense of well-being and belonging inside a group of *healthy*-minded peers, do great in school, make great memories (which I didn't in my rebellion), and then continue to excel after graduation and beyond. I wish I could say I made the right choices in school, but instead, I made some wrong choices regarding my friends, the places I went, and the things I did.

Then, peer pressure was added to the mix above, which existed in and out of school. That happens when you choose to conform or not conform to the social requests or demands (pressure) of others. And with that added peer pressure, you were either popular or not, or you hung around those who were popular or not. Your desire was to fit in somewhere inside a sea of students unless you wanted zero friends. Admittedly, that scenario became a real struggle for me—the fitting-in part. I would like to think it wasn't a problem, but it really was. The fitting in and where I would fit inside a massive body of students included both friends and enemies.

The enemy part I never went looking for. They found me, whether I liked it or not, and I can assure you that I never started anything. I don't have a mean streak in me. I'm more of a peacemaker. I didn't want a conflict with any peer; it just wasn't in my nature. The conflicts and peer pressure came unwanted anyhow. Ironically, it's part of navigating through high school, but I wasn't privy to that insight. When the conflicts and peer pressure kicked in, that would send my head reeling at times and tears running down my cheeks (always in secret, of course).

When it came to the largest groups, the *greatest* distinction between the cliques became those who obeyed the rules and did well in school and those who did not. The troublemakers were not about to conform to the school's standards—or anyone else's standards, for that matter.

They rebelled against the system; the troublemakers of the high school population were unwise, unruly, and deviant. And everyone knew about them, even when there was no social media, Facebook, or smartphones. In the seventies, word got around nonetheless.

Ironically, that was the group I got caught up in. I socially identified myself with that clique: the troublemakers. Don't laugh at that name. I didn't make it up. Someone else did. That also really wasn't the name of the group, but that name existed before my time and I borrowed it versus using the real name. The point is that I not only became twisted up in the wrong group and then belonged to it, that particular clique was altogether fickle. They either liked you or they didn't, and if they didn't, you knew about it, as you will soon read. Not ironically, at the heart of the clique was a culture of drugs and more.

Here I must add that we are not the sum of the labels we choose or that were placed upon us as I mentioned earlier. Those labels are not part our identity if we are following Christ. We can renew our minds by reading the Word and replacing labels with scriptures. Most of all, our true identity is in Christ, not in what others say about us or have done to us. Additionally, labels and sayings such as, "You're worthless," "You won't amount to anything," "You're stupid," or any other word or phrase that has hounded you in your head can be healed. The Lord can peel those words and phrases and the shame that comes with them right out of you. He can heal your fractured self and the way you see yourself. You just have to pray and ask and have faith for change. Then, dismantle the giant in your head—take it down. Take down the wrong labels and sayings and take back the land that the enemy has stolen: your unique identity and personality.

It says in 2 Corinthians 5:17, "Therefore, if anyone is in Christ, he is a new creation; old things have passed away; behold, all things have become new."

HERE COMES THE FAMILY MESS

A major family split was going to take place during those teenage years, and it appeared that my inner world was beginning to crumble while my parents' marriage fell apart. Divorce is hard on *everyone*. It's especially hard when you're told growing up that Christians shouldn't divorce and then they do, and it's even harder when it hits close to home. But that's not the point of this chapter, and many things can be said about this unfortunate subject. However, as an adult, I believe there are specific Bible verses and reasons as to why divorce would be applicable. All right, enough said for now. I'm trying not to go there. ... Yet, back in the seventies, there was a social stigma attached to divorcing Christians plus the added shame. It all seemed to fall on the children as well. How do I know? I was there. I was forced to watch and feel all the negativity surrounding a chaotic family breakup. I used to wear that social disgrace, and I also felt highly flawed and marginalized, even as a young person. (But without a doubt, God can heal the fracture that divorce creates.)

Early on, our family went to church several times a week, and we all participated in some capacity. My mother was a concert pianist and played for our church. My father was an usher. My sister, Donna, and I were part of many church youth groups while growing up, and we sang in the choir and traveled, both at school and at church. When our family began to disintegrate, we went to church less and less. Soon, we all quit going to church (for a season), and I stopped being a committed Christian. In other words, I backslid in a big way—but not initially.

As my parents fought more and more, that's when my dear grandmother suddenly moved away, and she meant the world to me. When that unforeseeable event happened, it was as if all family stability vanished before my eyes. In return, constant change stepped in. What I didn't know right away was why my grandparents left and went back to their hometown far away. Later I found out they left because they didn't want to watch our Christian family self-destruct. They also didn't want to watch my sister and I be torn apart during the fiasco. Adding to the drama, my sister and I separated. I am sure it would have been hard to watch (for anyone) as our family unit evaporated.

When that sorry saga began, both parents sought me out to ask me for information regarding each other on a continual basis. I felt used like a pawn and stuck in the middle of their debacle and squabbling and more. It was such a confusing mess as it became a he-said, she-said" campaign. Who was right, and who was wrong? Or was anyone right at all in that complicated mess? The mess only served to cloud my judgment and thinking. It also wasn't a good time at all for anyone, which meant no fun whatsoever for any of us. How could I know who was really right or wrong when I was trying to believe the best in both parents' stories? I didn't know where to place my alliance. That too is another subject in itself: when family members choose sides against one another. And, of course, I won't go there. That's another mess to walk through.

Anyhow, as a teen, I ended up listening to more than I want to share here, although I wanted to know the truth. That not knowing went on for years in my head, as I couldn't seem to find closure with their divorce mess. Still, I was ignorant to some things going on behind closed doors. (One day, I would find out more missing pieces to the puzzle.) However, when my new reality began to unfold during and after their divorce, everything I had been told while growing up (the good stuff), everything I believed was going to happen in my life (the fun stuff), and everything about my future that was ever promised just suddenly dissipated. It was totally gone. My promising future—the good stuff and the fun stuff—now became quite unsure and unpredictable as our family unit unraveled. Simply stated, given time, the dreams were gone. The dreams died. When their divorce was finally over, it left me feeling broken, abandoned, and rebellious. Plus, I am certain that my acting-out behavior (which was escalating) didn't help my parents during a difficult transition in life.

At that time, I didn't know what I know now: that God wants to heal and restore each one of us. Whether you were involved in a divorce or as a child you felt ripped apart during your parents' divorce, here is a verse to hold onto: "Though you have made me see troubles, many and bitter, you will restore my life again; from the depths of the earth you will again bring me up. You will increase my honor and comfort me once more (Ps. 71:20–21 NIV).

A NEW SOCIAL VIRUS

At the same time while in eighth grade, I was trying to have a sense of belonging and become a part of a group, but I couldn't seem to fit in with so many new students. Sure I had some friends from previous years, and sure I had just lost my BFF to my first love, Brad. Yet I began to notice that the guys liked me and the girls couldn't stand me. They really disliked me without a valid reason, which reminds me of a verse found in Psalms 69:4. It mentions that we can be hated without a cause. "Those who hate me without a cause are more than the hairs of my head; they are mighty who would destroy me, being my enemies wrongfully." And this verse became my firsthand experience—undeserved, just like the Bible says.

Truthfully, all I was trying to do was survive a new school and a brand-new social setting, which always seemed to be changing. This was especially true when the former eighth graders graduated to the high school building and the new seventh graders came on board the middle school. Right about then, I started hanging out with the wrong group of teens and began pressing limits on what I could and couldn't get away with. My behavior only served to get me in trouble at school and at home, and that led to an increase in detentions and suspensions (for the next several years), which didn't go over very well at home. And those consequences at school led to further consequences at home, including being grounded, being given extra chores to do, and losing privileges, like the phone.

It became easier to get away with more later on due to the changes within my family's dynamics. That defiance to rules, regulations, and academics increased little by little over time in my small world. My total lack of concern led me to do barely enough academically to get by in school (and prior to that I was an honor student), while I further experimented with drugs. Those choices went against my Christian upbringing, which I forfeited. I sought to numb myself to compensate for the pain of watching and listening to my parents' divorce drama and the ongoing conflicts at school. I know I'm not the only one who used drugs to cope, but I am not condoning my actions because there were repercussions for those wrong choices—regrettable ones. And it wasn't the right way to do life. There is a much better way to do life with Christ in it. He can help you overcome your troubles, regardless of your situation.

During that time, there was no internet frenzy boasting of substance abuse as can be read online today. Only by word of mouth did others boast among themselves of what they did in private or as a group. I didn't realize people would outright brag about their addictions online until I bumped into that dialogue while doing some research for this book. Back then, my drug use remained totally off the record—all done in secret and hidden from adults and some peers. Had I only turned to the Lord during my parents' divorce and the family breakup or during stressful times at school, He would have helped me walk through it. Instead, I did it my way—the long, hard way, the regrettable way.

In Psalms 41:7, it reads, "All who hate me whisper together against me; against me they devise my hurt." And the following story actually took place when others decided to gang up on me to unfriend me. It can be compared to the instant messaging of today's social media, whereby complete strangers and so-called friends tell you to go kill yourself, which you know is horrible, no-good advice. The only difference back then was their malevolent words were handwritten on paper and not fabricated on technology for all eyes to see.

Before the onset of the internet and smartphones, students used to pass notes back and forth to communicate. We would take notebook paper and fold it until it represented a triangular football. Some students would then punt their notes to their friends across the desks without saying a word. Self-contained messages and secrets were delivered via that little football. Remember, cell phones and instant messaging did not exist, which meant *no form* of social media existed as a platform to bully, but bullying existed just the same.

After school one day while I was walking home, I opened a rather large letter that I had received in class (and it was too thick to be folded like a football). Nonetheless, I saved the huge letter to read on my way home, so I could devote time to digest its contents. I thought it was all good, never dreaming it would contain the opposite. Generally, everyone gave notes or letters to each other throughout the course of the day. That was nothing new. However, when I opened mine, I had never seen or read a letter like the one I was about to read in my entire life. All of a sudden, it felt like the ground was shaking underneath my feet, only it was me shaking when I read their malicious words. Their words critically and emotionally wounded me. Although no one could see the wound, I sure felt the impact of their words ricochet throughout my being. I was surely unprepared for that sudden jolt to my emotions. Staggering as I walked (and I was completely sober, mind you), I was overcome with fear and dread as I read their threatening letter that was several pages long. Waves of tears and sobbing welled up inside me, rolling out of me, and I could barely see to read as my tears hit their letter. I was extremely traumatized by their complete and utter rejection of me. At fourteen, I was dumbfounded by reading hate mail (designed to cause harm) written by a group of mean girls, targeting their handwritten letter especially for me.

To top it off, it was Sharon who instigated the series of unfortunate events. She was able to manipulate a circle of girls (or a gang of girls, as some may say) to collectively and individually write a paragraph or an entire page or two about how much they couldn't stand me (and that's saying it rather nicely) *and* how they never wanted to be my friend ever again. It went beyond unfriending and bordered acts of intended violence. Imagine an entire group of adolescents despising someone, deploring me, and for what? Why me? What did I do? I had done nothing to offend any one of those girls, especially Sharon, whom I hardly knew and rarely saw.

When it comes to hate, I didn't know then, but I know now. They hated Jesus without a cause too—to the point that He was despised, betrayed, and killed. (See Isaiah 53:3 and Matthew 27.) He was blameless, and I'm the opposite—not perfect. I'm a sinner saved by grace. "For by grace you have been saved through faith, and that not of yourselves; it is the gift of God, not of works, lest anyone should boast" (Eph. 2:8–9). Yet, as a prodigal, as a rebellious teen, the Lord was watching over me, and the story wasn't over.

And still, there was more to come. Would it ever end? Unbelievably, Sharon, who was just an acquaintance from school, had a cousin in another school who turned out to be more of a threat as a bully than Sharon. You can read about her cousin in another chapter. Anyhow, the high school group that I was dealing with right then (the troublemakers) disliked everything about me, warning me to stay away from them and blatantly rejecting my developing self. They also warned me not talk to any of *our* guy friends—the guys they liked and I liked as friends. We all hung out together from time to time, but I was threatened that I could not be seen talking to the guys any longer, *or* they would come and beat me up. We were all friends, or so I believed until that happened. And yes, some of the girls had boyfriends, but I would have never liked their boyfriends. That kind of maladjusted behavior exchanged for my friendship broke me. Up to that point in time, I thought they were my friends.

And besides that, had I been walking with the Lord and learning about

Him, there may have been a different outcome, or I may have had different friends altogether. The Bible can point you in the right direction when it comes to having friends. There are friends who stick closer than a brother, and well, they weren't those kinds of friends. The other important point is that the Lord can heal our broken selves, including our mixed emotions, self-worth, and minds. In writing this, it reminds me of Joyce Meyer's book *Battlefield of the Mind*. Years ago, it brought me encouragement when I read it. It's a great read on right thinking.

To make matters worse, after reading their harassing letters, some of the girls (not guys) began circulating rumors and notes about me from class to class to class. Their made-up lies spread like wildfire with no internet in sight. That started when one of my so-called friends, really a nonfriend, got with her girlfriends (whom I didn't know) to spearhead a group of teens against me. I could have just keeled over, and I couldn't get my hands on their notes to stop it. Everyone in the school must have read those *fake* notes, as they were being passed around and grabbed out of other students' hands and then tossed to yet another student to read. So on and on went the girls' plan, and their scheme continued throughout the school. Their outlandish slander and gossip were similar to circulating false rumors on the internet today by using Facebook, Twitter, Instagram, or any other popular app to post messages that will discredit, humiliate, or wreak havoc in an individual's life to the point of suicide. That real-life event of the past was like the cyberbullying of today. It's terrible that people are taking their lives when there is an answer and there is a God who heals broken hearts. We just have to turn to Him. I've been there. That's why I'm bringing it up. He came to set us free from what others have said or done to us. No matter what happened, there is a better way out of the pain, and it's not substance abuse or suicide or hurting yourself. It's Christ. He's what the world still needs today.

When I heard and saw how incredibly cruel everyone was acting, it further destroyed me. It felt like the whole world knew those lies about me, and here it was a new school full of students that heard it all. That was hard to deal with. I was a virgin (which no one knew), but they fabricated notes and rumors telling my small world the complete opposite. They went on to spread the worst, most unimaginable kinds of things that I cannot put into print here. Their unjust behavior, deemed a social virus, spread so fast that

I couldn't seem to make the wrongs right. I couldn't prevent it or control it or defend myself against a mob. Their actions further left me feeling rejected, embarrassed, and ostracized—like an outcast. When the girls' horrendous lies and shameful labels were pinned on me and then posted throughout the school, I can only *compare* what was being said about me to this verse out of Ezekiel 16:30 (International Standard Version): "'How weak is your heart,' declares the Lord God, 'when you committed all of these deeds, the acts of an imperious whore!'"

When I went searching for a scripture to describe what was being spread about me (all the lies), I was surprised to find many verses in the Bible that mention a harlot. And I didn't know I could find such a verse to explain what they were saying about me until I searched the internet. Yet they called me that name and more in print and circulated it. I never wanted anyone to view me or judge me like that, especially the boys in the school. … Regardless of anyone's actions, I was none of what they were accusing me of. I was nothing like what the above verse describes. Today it is nicknamed an entirely different type of shaming that I won't put into print here. However, the damage was done, and that left me feeling alienated by the added gawkers, who shamefully ridiculed me for being someone or something I wasn't. Being bullied by a mob at school and hounded by their continuous mocking lies served to not only terrorize me but cause me to emotionally withdraw and shut down. I regressed into an unjustified, disgraced silence. I had been there before when I was called a slew of fat-shaming names, and I never thought I would see that social injustice again.

The Word is full of life and help to all who are in need, and these two verses are both a reminder and a blessing to know: "'For I will restore health to you and heal you of your wounds,' says the Lord, 'Because they called you an outcast saying: 'This is Zion; No one seeks her'" (Jer. 30:17–20). And: "Do not fear, for you will not be ashamed; neither be disgraced, for you will not be put to shame; for you will forget the shame of your youth" (Is. 54:4). How good and how awesome is the Lord to heal and restore us, thereby bringing us back to life even after others have despitefully tried to ruin us!

THE AFTERMATH

In looking back, were they jealous? I never could understand jealousy, and I'm not a jealous person. Jealousy is hateful, hurtful, and vengeful. It also drives people apart. Nonetheless, rejection persecuted me, and slander spit in my face. Everything I was becoming as a blossoming young girl was being torn apart. Although it appeared as if the other girls my age were having the time of their lives, I just couldn't seem to compete with that. The impact it had on my self-esteem was altogether crippling. *Every day* I had to face the music—my accusers—and the music wasn't pretty. I detested going to school because of what took place. Plus, I felt overwhelmed facing another day at school and disliked being there after that year. But I went regardless of what I faced and persevered against the firestorm of fear, their threats, and verbal assaults.

The hostility that filled the air was hard to comprehend. I had never been subject to such animosity and malice coming from what I thought were my girlfriends. I saw myself as kind and easy to get along with, but that apparently was not a good fit with the group. I wasn't mean, cruel, or thoughtless. Was it because of the new me? Remember, I had worked to change my appearance and dropped the weight. It was like the story of the ugly duckling turning into a beautiful swan, only I still felt ugly on the inside, being stuck in that toxic mess at school, and I couldn't seem to escape it. In the past, I had been bullied and rejected for being overweight and ran home in tears. In reflection, was I being bullied for changing? Had the transformation that I labored for provoked a new type of bullying—one I wasn't prepared for obviously? And who would be? It was tragic, and I couldn't shake it off overnight. But one day I would. The entire experience crushed me until I got my heart right with the Lord. He gave me beauty for ashes!

The clique's abusiveness and mean-spirited accusations were completely unwarranted and false. Stunned, I was on their chopping block. And just like that, I had a whole bunch of female enemies against me, and for what? I couldn't or wouldn't hurt anyone, like I said. Their words, whether by mouth or in print, ruined me for a long time. How was I going to cope? How was I going to handle that group? What should I do? I couldn't quit school. It wasn't an option, and there was no homeschooling. Who could

I talk to? Nobody discussed student culture issues or abnormal behavior. Today, it is openly discussed and on trend. Today, there is help if someone is being bullied or abused. Back then, I didn't open up to my parents or anyone. Not much was available to turn to, especially resources. Today, it's not only talked about, but there is support available everywhere you turn. As a teen in the seventies, I felt isolated, as my social skills weren't mature enough to handle being bullied by a group of girls. So instead, I wept in private and buried the trauma inside my heart as I cried myself to sleep and numbed my pain with drugs.

At that point, I wasn't a Christian and I wasn't living for the Lord. I dealt with being afraid to go to school, and I allowed my grades to suffer because I was busy watching my back and coping with life at home. Every day I was afraid to face my accusers, yet we were all in the same building. I wasn't quite sure how to defend myself against so many *mean* girls, as I was no match for them. If I told anyone and the word circulated back to those girls, they would have ganged up on me during school, walking home after school, or in any public place. How do I know about those threats? They warned me that I had better keep my mouth shut.

However, a positive outcome to the peer pressure and mob bullying was in sight. I became determined to make a new group of friends, to surround myself with them, and to move forward little by little. Out of that trial, God had His hand on me—a prodigal.

IN CONCLUSION
MOB BULLYING DID NOT DEFINE ME

The good news is that after rededicating my life to Jesus Christ, I attended a huge Christian outdoor festival. Out of the Jesus movement of the late sixties and seventies sprang enormous festivals that brought anywhere from ten thousand to eighty thousand people in attendance, spanning across the United States and beyond. I went to many of those festivals after I became a Christian, as they impacted my life in a tremendous, unforgettable way. Plus, I was able to meet people from all over the world who were hungry to *know* the Lord. The power of the Lord was manifest during those gatherings of young and old alike. It was during one of those events that the Lord was digging deeper inside of me, freeing me from the pain of the past. In the meeting, we were asked to forgive anyone who has hurt us, and it was at that point I forgave the girls of all the things they said or did.

Afterward, I received a breakthrough, experiencing inner healing and a release from the past. By the end of the weekend, I returned home happy, full of joy, and free of the painful memories. Honestly, I know the Lord can free a person from what's bothering them, whether it takes place at a huge outdoor festival, on the internet, inside a church, at home, or in a prison cell. Nothing shall separate us from the love of Christ. (See Romans 8:35–39.) Also, know that He shows no partiality, which means one person is not better than another. That being true, in regard to what the Lord has done inside my heart, He wants to do the same for you. He wants to bring about healing and restoration in each one of our lives.

> Then they cried out to the Lord in their trouble, and He saved them out of their distresses. He sent His word and healed them, and delivered them from their destructions.
> — Psalms 107:19–20

> Fear not, for I am with you; be not dismayed, for I am your God. I will strengthen you, yes, I will help you, I will uphold you with My righteous right hand.
> — Isaiah 41:10

> Instead of your shame you shall have double honor, and instead of confusion they shall rejoice in their portion. Therefore, in their land they shall possess double; everlasting joy shall be theirs.
> — Isaiah 61:7

CHAPTER 6

STEALING AND THE BULLY

If someone treats you bad, just remember that there is something wrong with them, not you. Normal people don't go around destroying other people. Never let someone with the significance of a speed bump become a road block in your life!

—http://www.lessonslearnedinlife.com

School was out for the summer, and I had just turned fifteen, but at fifteen, I wanted to work. The only way to get a job was to lie about my age. You had to be sixteen in order to apply for a job. So I inappropriately lied. If I wanted the extras in life—lots of clothes and all of the girly things, plus money for pot—I needed to find outside employment. And because I wasn't serving the Lord (at least not yet), I justified the lie. After the initial employment interview, I was hired on the spot. It was exciting to know that I would have money coming in to spend and spend. My first job as a carhop was close to home yet far enough away that I couldn't walk. I became a carhop (waitress) for the P & K Drive-In franchise, which had its beginning in outside, curbside service dating way back to the roaring twenties. Eventually, the chain grew to well over 1,700 restaurants, as it became that popular throughout the United States. And no, I never delivered food in roller skates like other drive-in chains.

As a carhop, I would run over and place a ticket on the patron's windshield after they parked their car under the canopy. In return, they would turn on their headlights to get service or when they were ready to leave. Once service was provided, they turned their lights off. The constant running around kept me slim as I ran from car to car. To get to work, I either rode a bike, caught a ride from a friend, or was dropped off and picked up by my mom. In other words, I needed to be resourceful in getting to and from work because I was too young to drive. On a side note, the root beer was in such high demand that soon the P & K Distributing Company was born, and they became a nationally recognized beverage in the grocery store aisle. Today, their restaurant franchises are no longer in operation, although they originally made some of the best tasting root beer around. There was nothing like downing a chilled, frosty glass mug of ice-cold root beer, loaded with lots of foam on top! I wouldn't drink one today, but I can assure you, I enjoyed loads of them back in the day, especially a frothy root beer float filled with vanilla ice cream.

To keep up with my drug binging, someone at work showed me how and when to steal money before it hit the cash register and was counted. You would think I would have thought that one through first, before I tried to get away with it. You would think that my conscious would have convicted me and the consequences would scare me, but addicts do not think of all those truths. They take the dare instead. You know … truth or dare. Drugs pollute your thinking skills, and drugs were the motive behind my stealing. So my thinking was clearly messed up. My conscious was clogged because I didn't want to own the wrong that I was doing, and I was rebelling against the Lord's ways, like a prodigal. Recall the prodigal in the book of Luke, chapter 15? The prodigal son squandered his inheritance (his money and his youth) doing all the wrong things. And that's exactly what I was doing until I got to the end of myself, just like he did.

Yet, until that day arrived in my life, someone at work explained to me how the tally system was used. Everyone who worked there submitted numbered paper receipts after the food was delivered and monies exchanged. Nothing was digital. Today, you can scan receipts, or food is ordered digitally, but back then, it was manually written down, and paper records were kept. The old cash register they used was outdated and obsolete, and eventually a sloppy bookkeeping rumor surfaced. It was the job of the manager on duty to sequence all the receipts at the end of the workday. That vital task usually remained undone, and word got around. After I learned what to do, I stole from the owner. Large-ticket receipts disappeared along with the money, as they were never handed over as instructed. Not only did I live in fear of being found out, but I used the stolen money to supply my drug habit beyond a paycheck and any tips. Certainly, I'm not proud to admit to stealing (or using), but drugs impact your thinking. *It takes a thief* to supply a drug habit, especially when you are out of funds and the cost to binge is higher than what you earn. You might think you will never do that, but then you do. As an addict, you'd be surprised at how low you'd go.

In the future, my past actions would somehow remind me of the two thieves (criminals) who hung upon crosses, one on each side of Jesus, who himself was hanging upon a cross at Calvary. One blasphemed Jesus; the other one rebuked him and defended the Lord. "Then he said to Jesus, 'Lord, remember me when You come in Your kingdom!' And Jesus said to him, 'Assuredly, I say to you, today you shall be with me in Paradise'" (Luke 23:42–43). What forgiveness Jesus bestowed on the thief who hung on the cross. This passage always moves me to tears, as I once considered myself to be like the thief who was remorseful and gained forgiveness for the sins he committed. That was mercy and forgiveness and the beauty of pure love.

For the most part in eighth grade and during my freshman year, one of the mean girls in high school, whom I tried to get along with, appeared to have a split personality. In my opinion back then, *nothing* ever made her happy, and she was rarely in a good mood. If you weren't Sharon's best friend or on her good side that day, she could become reckless and flip out on you; friend or not, it didn't seem to matter. When her personality switched to the one you didn't want to be near, watch out; you were back to not being her friend. Even her best friends came and went. If she hurt you, it never seemed to bother her. Most of the time I couldn't tell which personality she was going to exhibit when I walked inside the school building. Would she be naughty or nice? Sharon liked to bully others and was always looking for a fight. If her goal was to make you afraid of her, she achieved it some of the time. She must have thrived off the attention and drama it created. You couldn't help but notice.

For me, I seldom knew what she was going to say or do when I got near her. She had an inner circle of girlfriends who joined in on her antics at school, and I tried to avoid them as much as possible, but some of our friends overlapped. Otherwise, I would have avoided her altogether. It was not a good friend setup whatsoever. What was missing were all the elements that make for a great friendship—you know, the good things, like trust, honesty, and integrity. Sharon was the one who had her hand in instigating a gang of girls to write the infamous letter containing threats and intended violence directed toward me. That letter was extremely similar to cyberbullying, except for their words weren't stuck inside some virtual cloud for all eyes to see. Their words once in print and on notebook paper have long since turned to dust. The rotten, streaming letter was aimed to stop me from talking to any guy she knew or her friends knew in eighth grade. Innocently, I was just talking to guys—not a thing more, as I had said before. And to think, we were never close friends, just acquaintances, if that. It was a real ordeal dealing with her and her friends. With all of that taking place, my new boundaries became social distancing and learning to work around them in order to get through a day at school. Incidentally, no one ever mentioned social distancing back in the day.

Anyhow, Sharon had a cousin who was an upperclassman. And if I thought Sharon was a bully to be reckoned with, then her older cousin, whom I would soon meet, was a sheer terror. I could hardly believe that a female could become so coldhearted and intimidating. Her cousin could easily fit the description of a bully times ten. It was sad to realize that I would have more to deal with in trying to get an education *and* work my first job. It had been a rude awakening for me to deal with those two contentious females. Where was the playbook on how to play the game with the twisted cousins? There wasn't any. It was beyond me. It takes a lot of energy to be a bully. What made the twisted cousins act so unkind and adversarial? Where did they learn that type of misbehavior? What made them so antisocial? Where was it coming from? I was just trying to survive high school, and it was severe enough that I wanted to quit school a hundred different times, but I didn't. I'm pleased I didn't quit school.

At first, I was happy to have a job, but once I met Denise, the cousin, everything changed overnight. Her demeanor was brutish. She reminded me of an untamed wild dog. I didn't know Denise and wished I never had to meet her. She did not attend my high school but a senior high in another part of town. At least that was in my favor. However, when school was out, she did wind up finding the exact same job at the P & K that I had, and I was about to meet her for the very first time. Imagine that. No, don't imagine; read on.

When I first met Denise at work, she sent shivers down my spine. Honestly, I did not have a good feeling about her when we first saw each other. I was scared stiff, but I would *never* let that be known. Later in the day, I sat with my head in my hands, thinking, *What am I going to do now? Why would she lunge at me as she walks by?* And that is exactly what she did from time to time. I didn't lunge back at her because I was at work and it wasn't in my nature. I also lacked some training on how to deal with unbelievably difficult people at the age of fifteen. I had always wished that I had an older brother. What would he have done in a situation like that? I can only surmise. But if I had a brother, he would have probably given me some helpful suggestions to try. Yet I continued to ponder, *What did I ever do to her? I've done nothing to hurt her! I don't even know the person who just walked into my life. Soon, she'll know that I go to the same school as her cousin, and she may put two and two together. But for now, I'm not going to volunteer who I know and don't know. That will buy me some time. How much time? I'm not sure.*

In looking way back, I was never a bully, yet I was bullied. I'll never understand why people spend time tearing others down. There are better things to aim for in life, such as do good to others and use the Golden Rule, which is found in Matthew 7:12. Life doesn't always treat us well because it's not a perfect world—not yet. It's what you do with what you know in the end that counts: forgive, overcome, and press forward as you follow Christ. Plus, embrace the fruits of the spirit, which are found in Galatians 5:22–23: "But the fruit of the Spirit is love, joy, peace, longsuffering, kindness, goodness, faithfulness, gentleness, self-control." Well, at the time, I didn't accept these scriptures or try to walk them out because, as you can read, I wasn't a sold-out believer. In the future, I made it a heartfelt goal by reading the Word and trying to apply it as best as possible. Not only did I want to change for the better later, but by choosing to be around other like-minded Christians, we could help each other out and do life better together.

Although I wasn't close to Sharon, even in a group setting it was totally fake for us as friends. In other words, what a phony friendship. For the most part, I stayed out of her path and out of her face at school. Then, over time, I tried everything I could think of—avoid her, ignore her, befriend her, and fake it till I made it—but in the end I survived. However, I was still caught in a totally new predicament. There were now two females who really didn't know me, yet I was forced to work alongside someone who could become quite unpredictable and volatile. And soon, Denise would know that I knew Sharon. Then it occurred to me once more: *It's only a matter of time. Maybe I have only a few hours or a couple of days or quite possibly she'll know tomorrow.* And what's more was she would eventually know that Sharon didn't like me—really, despised me—for whatever reason was in her head. Unbelievably, it was over someone's superficial opinion of me. Was she judging me by my outward appearance? It didn't make any sense to me at all. Even the Bible says, "Do not judge according to appearance, but judge with righteous judgement" (John 7:24). So that contrived contention between us was merely fiction in my eyes. It couldn't be real. She had conjured up an opinion based on what? Anyhow, I still had to work through the drama, like it or not. After meeting Denise, dread and fear struck me sideways (and that was real), as there was a new bully in town to contend with. Whether I liked it or not, I had to deal with it.

The only way I can tell this story is that when Denise finally found out I knew her cousin, she abruptly ran over to me at work and literally sneered in my face like a dog that was ready to devour its prey. The way I see it, attack dogs growl and bark, they change their posture, and their hair stands up, and that is exactly what happened. Only, I'm talking about a real bully trying to mark her territory, like a dog that marks its territory. Let me add that I'm not calling her a dog. It was that her actions actually reminded me of a dog gone wild. When Denise would come near me, she would intentionally stomp her feet, then lunge forward to strike me, and then threaten to come and get me so she could beat me up. "I'm going to get you," she would say under her breath. "It's not a matter of if I'm gonna get you; it's a matter of when I'm going to beat you up."

Over time, Denise would add to her threats and then repeat those threats to my face. She would often take her clenched fist and smack her fist into her other hand in front of me and say, "This is for you." Not only did that cause fear to mount, but panic set in as I cringed inside. Sometimes she would rush up on me and then stop herself before an actual face-off occurred. Of course, it left me feeling petrified, shaken, and overwhelmed. Besides trying to fake it till I made it while at work, I tried all of the above again to survive. And the taunting continued as I had to walk past her while we waited on cars together. I smiled at my customers (with my fake smile) like everything was OK when it was anything but that. The apprehension of going to work was followed by the thought of, *Is she on the clock? What awaits me if she is working?* That ruined my first job experience, yet I didn't quit when the going became super rough and stayed the entire season.

Bullying was never a topic of discussion while growing up—in books, at home, in church, or at school. The subject wasn't given much credence, but there were bullies. Today, it's the opposite. On all platforms, you may see or hear about a bully. Before social media existed, we were never encouraged to yell and tell a soul. There has been a huge paradigm shift for the better when it comes to communication and available resources about an unavoidable topic of dealing with a bully.

In looking back on those incidents, I know that God in His supreme kindness was watching out for His prodigal child, and one day I would find my way back to Him.

Thankfully, in the above situation, there was an open door out of the craziness. It came through another coworker who worked alongside of me. Michelle was a part of a military ROTC program while attending a local university. As a young cadet, she both befriended and mentored me. I believe she was sent into my life for such a time as that situation, bringing an intervention. Even while I was a rebellious teen, the Lord was watching over me, and I can see His hand moving when I look back. What a lifesaver and Savior our Lord is. Furthermore, I believe Michelle was sent into my life for that reason. We instituted a buddy system at work. The first recorded buddy system dates back to 1942. The military made use of that strategy in World War II. That useful strategy brought a new friend into my life who helped me to survive the bully. And again, that buddy system provided relief from group bullying in the future when *other* upperclassmen came to attack me with a knife in the suburbs. Imagine that. The Lord spared me, but you can read about this next. It really helped going forward to know that two heads are better than one, both at work and at school.

Michelle was older, more experienced, and more the size of the bully than I was. I was more of an introvert and quite petite. Her coaching skills and interest in me during a difficult time inspired me to survive my first job. I'm grateful she was there as a mentor. After that summer, I did not return back to the P & K when school let out the following year. Life moved on, so did my friend, and so did I. Let me leave you with this verse out of Ecclesiastes 4:9–10: "Two are better than one, because they have a good reward for their labor. For if they fall, one will lift up his companion. But woe to him who is alone when he falls, for he has no one to help him up." We can be better together, and there is strength in numbers.

IN CONCLUSION

One good way I survived being bullied at work was the buddy system. The second way was *not so smart*. How did I emotionally deal with that type of overt bullying and mental turmoil at fifteen? Instead of turning to the Lord *first* in prayer (whom I shut out of my head and my heart), I stuffed the pain down inside and numbed myself by doing drugs. That was to not feel the agony of being bullied at work and at school by the twisted cousins. Their rage against me was ongoing for a few years. It made life difficult to handle, being that I had to hear their constant threats and watch my back. I wasn't always sure how to overcome those dilemmas and didn't think that anyone would listen. It stretched way beyond girls being catty, and I had no proof without a smartphone to videotape their hostile actions like people can today. Additionally, there were no programs available in the seventies to access for help. Now, there are numerous safe places established to find help or assistance, which is wonderful, in addition to the technology that is available.

The second way I survived being bullied was *not* the answer either, which was by getting high. That destructive behavior did not solve any problem whatsoever, although that addiction created problems in itself. Plus, the problem, any problem, still existed when I was sober. In essence, you can't hide from your problems. Also, getting high didn't take away the bullies. It only *delayed* any viable solution, while it masked a developing issue—my secret addiction. This all changed in the future when I turned to the Lord.

And remember the stealing? To right a wrong after I became a Christian in my late teens, I stopped by to deliver a letter of apology to the owner of the P & K Drive-In. It was to say, "I'm sorry for stealing your money. My life has changed. … I asked Jesus in my heart." I never received a written reply. Then later, we spoke by phone, and the owner let it go and forgave me. Perhaps, in fact, that was mercy over the reality of what could have happened. The owner had the opportunity to file charges against me in juvenile court, and I could have possibly been sentenced, but I wasn't. That's when, "Mercy triumphs over judgment" (James 2:13). This was indeed the mercy of the Lord in my life versus judgment.

The Lord knows each one of us and the pain we carry, and He knows what has happened to us along the way. He is near to anyone who feels crushed by life, and He hears our cries. Jesus was afflicted, bruised, and broken for our sins. He paid the ultimate price for us on the cross. Ask Him to take away your pain, any injustice, and your suffering and then lay it at His feet beneath the cross in prayer. Ask Him to heal you in your innermost being. Forgive those who have harmed you, maliciously said all manner of evil against you, or have threatened your life. "Ask, and it will be given to you; seek, and you will find; knock, and it will be opened to you. For everyone who asks receives, and he who seeks finds, and to him who knocks it will be opened" (Matt. 7:7–8). Jesus will comfort the brokenhearted. He can heal the trauma that took place deep inside, and He can deliver anyone from any addiction. He came to set us free. Jesus can bring us total freedom from our past in order to be free to run the race set before us.

In looking over the Keys to Forgiveness Scale in Appendix I for example, I gave the above experience a three or four, which means it was harder to forgive, yet I forgave and let go. One reason I chose forgiveness is that Christ who lives in me can use me to touch others. I know He wants to liberate us so in return we can share this abundant life from Him with others. He often uses people like you and I to do this. You can also find in Appendix II helpful Strategies for Overcoming a bully, abuse, or addiction.

> And whenever you stand praying, forgive, if ye have anything against anyone, forgive him, that your Father in heaven may forgive you your trespasses. But if you do not forgive, neither will your Father in heaven forgive your trespasses.
>
> — Mark 11:25–26

CHAPTER 7

UNBELIEVABLY, THEY CAME WITH A KNIFE

There will always be people in your life who treat you wrong. Be sure to thank them for making you strong.

— Zig Ziglar

After graduating from middle school, the ninth and tenth graders were transported to an entirely different city. Located not in the inner city, mind you, but in middle-class suburbia where new residential developments were under construction. In that high school, I had new friends and old friends, both male and female. James was a friend of mine from middle school, and we constantly joked around together. We had met in seventh grade, and nothing ever developed between us. We remained strictly platonic friends. The friend part is important because, once more, it is about to be challenged. He was more like a brother to me—the brother I never had. I used to joke around with him and punch him in the arm in the hallway, jesting in-between classes.

Anyhow, James started dating an upper classmate in another school. I never met her, and he didn't tell me about her. So he and I were not that close, or I would have known about that detail. The very next thing I do know is that I received a message from *her* through someone else I didn't know either (but they both knew about of me). She said, "Trish is out to get you, and she wants to beat you up!"

You're kidding me, right? Is this some kind of joke? Those were my first two thoughts, followed by my reply. "Trish is after me for what? What did I do? Who's Trish anyhow? What class is she in? What school does she go to? I don't even know her, and I've never met her. How does she even know what I look like? How could she know me? Who told her what?" All those thoughts and more began running through my brain and out my mouth. And then I was left feeling puzzled, nervous, and fearful, which was all wrapped up into one sick, oozing mess: me. Is that a déjà vu experience or what? It felt like I had been there before. Honestly, I was about to be bullied for joking with my friend—a male friend. C'mon now. I couldn't believe it was happening again. What was it with some girls? What happened to being nice? Certainly, I didn't want to live through that sort of drama ever again. There's more to life than bullying.

The news flash … Trish wanted to beat me up for saying hi to her boyfriend, my friend, James.

HOME ALONE

After arriving home from school, I noticed my mom wasn't home, so I was home alone. Sometimes she stayed after work, and I would arrive home first, which was what happened on the day I had unannounced visitors. At the time, we lived in a six-unit apartment complex in a small, quaint suburb. Mom was single and divorced and worked full time. When she wasn't home, on occasion, I took full advantage of my freedom. And because she wasn't home, I decided to get high in the house after school. Again, I wasn't living for the Lord. Furthermore, by that time, I was completely noncompliant and rebellious, busy doing my own thing and mostly answering to no one. Getting stoned by me was no big deal, whether it was morning, noon, or night. Besides, I was alone. Who would care? I didn't care.

Anyhow, I had just finished smoking a joint and was beginning to feel the effects of it when I heard someone knocking loudly at the door. Candidly, I was all of 105 pounds, give or take, and about five four, which was kind of skinny and no match for whoever was beyond the door. And to top it off, our doors didn't have any peepholes installed in order to see who was beyond the door. I never inquired who was at the door, which meant I didn't take the time to ask these key proverbial phrases: "Hello, who is it?" "Who's at the door?" "Who's knocking?" You know, the type of questions that protect you from unwanted intruders. That was a seriously bad move on my part, as I was in the moment and feeling rather buzzed and melancholy when I swung the door open and looked up. Had there been a peephole in the door to look through, it would have given me a heads-up to *not* open the door. I wish there had been a Ring or SimpliSafe security system installed or any sort of webcam device enabled to save me by recording the intrusion, but none of that existed. Instead, after I swung open the door, my first thought became, *Oh, this isn't good. I'm in imminent danger.* Instantly, I became sober, hypervigilant, and hyperalert. My heart was pounding, as if I could hear my heart echoing in the hallway. I felt myself becoming stiff, unsmiling, and straight-faced.

When I looked up, there were three very tall, large, angry looking girls standing right in front of me. I had not one or two but three older females against me. I sort of recognized one of them, but I still didn't know her, and the other two I had never seen before in my life. The one in the middle immediately stuck her foot in the door to block the doorway, so I couldn't shut the door. Staring down at me, she said, "Do you know me? You're gonna know me by the time I'm finished with you." Then she announced, "I'm James's girlfriend."

Immediately, it dawned on me who she was and what was about to go down. Furthermore, she had been stalking me and found out where I lived. Who told her where I lived anyhow? As I was digesting everything taking place in front of me, I'm not sure which I saw first, her face or the knife. In her fist she held a knife; it looked like a long butcher knife. I couldn't help but flinch inside as I tried not to look at it and its blade as I thought about what might happen. Only after she began smacking the knife against the palm of her hand did I freeze up inside, knowing I couldn't run into the house or move away from the door, especially with her big foot stuck in the doorway.

At that point, Trish threatened me. "I've come to let you have it." Then she asked me, "Is anybody else here?"

Fumbling for my words, I said, "Yes, my mom."

She quickly asked, "Really? Where's your mom?"

"She's in the bathroom taking a bath," I managed to get that out of my mouth, wondering what to say next as I stood there stone-faced.

Trish didn't waste any time, replying, "Well, if she's here, have her call out. Have her say something! We're waiting."

Pausing to stall for time, my only hope was that someone would walk through the apartment entrance and rescue me. *Where is everybody?* I wondered. *Where is everyone in the building anyway? It's time for people to start coming home from work.* I also knew that the lie about my mom in the bath wasn't about to work because she truly wasn't home, and I knew it. I was just deliberately trying to buy time, and nothing was working. Then, because that idea was falling apart, I admitted the truth. "She's not home," I said, "but I expect her any minute."

I kept my eyes glued on Trish, staring back at her while she stood glaring at me. Our eyes were locked. As I kept my eyes glued on hers, my left hand was visible and holding the door between us, while my right hand was behind the door beginning to quietly set the lock and hoping the lock couldn't be heard by anyone or it was all over. I thought to myself, *I'll only have one chance to save myself. It's three against me.* That was not a good situation. I stood there emotionless and observing Trish.

She said, "We went to every door in this building and knocked on each door, and no one is home! Now, this leaves just the four of us."

Can you believe that? *Oh great! What am I going to do now?* I wondered. Then I began praying. The prodigal child was praying quietly in her head, *Lord, help me!*

The seconds felt like hours creeping by as Trish kept tapping her foot against the floor. Outwardly, she was getting restless. Then she went on to say, "I'm going to count." I can't remember if she said she was going to count to three, five, or ten because I was so panic-stricken and trying to stay focused at the same time. However, she did say, "I'm going to count, and when I'm done, you'd better come out, or we are going to drag you out." And I definitely heard that part.

Methodically, as if I had lots of time to stand around, I began waiting for the exact time to act. I was aware that I would have only *one* chance to save myself as I tried to push past the shock that was settling in. The sixty-second wait was beyond intense. As I looked at her, I was preparing to slam the door shut which had been previously locked. I would only have one opportunity. If they caught on and rushed the door, it would be over. There was no telling what they were capable of. ... And I was trying not to think of anything like the worst-possible case scenario you could live through in those last seconds. Those dreaded thoughts were not going to help me escape the crisis at hand.

When her eyes looked away from mine, for a split second, she glanced down at the floor. It was at that *priceless* moment that I heard a voice inside my head loudly saying, *Now!* I didn't realize it was Him, although I knew later it had to be the Lord. There's not a doubt in my mind that He spared me. He intervened and saved me. He *loved* the rebel, me, a prodigal. Instantly, when I heard the word *now*, I slammed the door shut, grabbed the chain above, put the chain on the door, and locked it as well.

For a second, I stood safe behind the door, wondering, *Can they break the door down?* That's when I heard lots of screaming, followed by the sound of their bodies slamming against the door and their fists pounding to get in. Next, I could hear someone carving on the door with the butcher knife they meant for me. Without hesitating, I ran into my bedroom and locked that door too. The worst thing was there was no 911 to call in the seventies. Certainly, there were no cell phones. To make matters worse, I didn't have the police number in front of me. Where was it? Where was the phone book? I hardly had time for any of it, but in my room there was a phone. Shaking, all I could remember was the phone number of the family across the street, and that was because my mother had me memorize their phone number just in case there was ever an emergency. More than ever, that counted as a huge emergency. As the phone began to ring, my heart was racing, and my thoughts turned to, *I hope someone's home. I hope somebody picks up the phone. Hurry up, please anyone pickup.* I was trying not to panic, but I was having a complete meltdown.

THANKFULLY, THE POLICE RESPOND

I'm grateful to the mother who was home when I called. She picked up the phone. By then, I was overwhelmed and trembling as I tried to blurt everything out to her over the phone. In return, my neighbor directly called the police. At that point, the girls threw the knife in the bushes, and the three of them ran off when they saw the police cruiser. When the police began to search the premises, they indeed found the knife. Their discovery took place while I waited at my neighbor's house, trying to pull myself together. Still, my mother wasn't home, and there was no way to reach her. Everyone assumed that she was on her way home from work. Was she running errands? Why was she running so late? How would I know if she wanted to stop at the store after work? Or was she getting her hair done? I couldn't say for sure where she was. Maybe, she was stuck in traffic. I'm only guessing. That was not a good day to run errands anywhere, but how would she know? There was no phone in the car, no cell phone, no communication, just plain, old dead air. Finally, when she arrived home, the police were still waiting, and they requested that we come down to the station and file a report. Needless to say, it was a long night.

As we filed a paper affidavit, I became fearful of pressing charges against the trio. That was when I asked my mom not to press charges. Nonetheless, a restraining order was placed on Trish, and it wasn't her first, so we were told. Honestly, I was not afraid of the court process but rather the repercussions that might transpire at school or elsewhere *if* I did make court a big deal. It was a gigantic deal either way. Whether we took the girls with the knife to court or I faced them on the streets, both placed me in jeopardy. Most of all, I didn't want to broadcast our experience to anyone I knew or they knew, as to not stir things up.

"There are already affidavits out on this girl," the policeman had indicated. Also, the officer noted Trish was not to be near me or seen near me, or we would press charges against her in the future if needed. Unbelievably, I returned to school the following day. To face what? I wasn't sure. Still, I can't believe to this day that I went back to school the very next day. My only solace was to know the trio did not attend my high school.

Privately, I was mortified of what those three upper classmates might be capable of doing. But I kept telling myself, *They're in another building in another part of town, and I'm safe.* Ironically, I didn't believe myself. I wanted to, but I couldn't seem to get there. Young and nearly sixteen, by then I was in tenth grade. Instead of excelling in school, I was always watching my back and watching where I went. That was because they further threatened my life, warning me by saying, "This isn't over. We're not through with you yet. It's only a matter of time." This is similar to the threats people make to others today on social media or just by walking down the street. The largest difference between then and now is that bringing weapons to school has dramatically increased. Rarely did you hear of females carrying a weapon to someone's house or to school back in the day, and now (sadly) that has changed drastically. Perhaps, that is another reason why I swung the door open. I wasn't worried about who was behind the door. Honestly, I would have never thought that I could be in peril at home or that I was being stalked. I couldn't have dreamt that a teenage girl would carry a weapon. It wasn't that I was completely naïve, but it was unheard of in the suburban neighborhood in which we resided. Once upon a time, people used to leave their doors unlocked, and now that is unheard of.

They were still out to get me regardless of any law, judicial system, or affidavit. Knife or no knife, they weren't about to stop their behavior. They didn't really care. I did. Afterward, my only plan was to keep friends nearby just in case *we* met face-to-face. My friends and I incorporated another buddy system to get through each day safely—not just one or two but many watching out for each other. And to cover up a little more pain, I delved deeper into the world of drugs. That part was *not* a good plan or a fitting solution for an ongoing dilemma.

You would think that because the Lord rescued and spared me and I knew it that I would change but I didn't—not then, not yet. I hadn't had enough. Except how could I ever forget the goodness of the Lord reaching out to me in that crisis, thereby sparing my life?

Being bullied for having a guy as a friend was at the least a letdown and at the most horrific. However, it was not the first time I was bullied for having a guy friend in high school. Soon, as you might guess, there was no more James. We spoke one last time. He said, "I can't believe that happened to you. I'm sorry." That sounded awfully nice to hear when he opened up, and that's all that was ever shared. The friendship was over. We both needed to move forward. Actually, what could he do about it? It looked like he had only a couple of choices: either talk to her or ditch her (you know, break up with her) for behaving like that. Well, eventually, James did the latter. So after our conversation was over, I unfriended him. Plus, his family moved far away. To where, I'll never know, and yet I wasn't sorry to see him go. Besides, that appeared to solve the entire boyfriend, guy-friend issue once and for all.

THE WRONG CROWD

After that major life event, my girlfriends at school surrounded me. But I must add, it was the wrong group of females. Here, I'm talking about the kind of girls who would stab you in the back on a moment's notice, the two-faced girlfriend type, not thoroughly genuine or trustworthy. And you couldn't tell if they were here today or gone tomorrow. For the time being, no one wanted me to be alone, and those were the girls who surrounded me both going and coming to school. So I had to take it at face value. Friend or foe, they were there watching out for me, which I surely appreciated, and that gave me some sense of safety, knowing there is safety in numbers.

Once more, that led to identifying with teenagers based upon the drug culture, although I did try to remove myself from being in the wrong group on more than one occasion. When a new school year would begin, I sought out an entirely different people group or clique, but I soon succumbed to the same group of guys and gals who I hung out with in eighth grade, nicknamed the troublemakers. That was due to the hold drugs had on me, and that addiction was ruining my life. The girls who hurt me so badly back in middle school were also in that group. It appeared I could not find my niche inside a sea of fickle girls. It was now those girls who protected me from the new bullies, the trio. Imagine that. Together, we smoked pot, partied with illicit drugs, became truant, and got into various degrees of trouble (hence, the troublemakers). We were not a good friend fit for each other in the long run, but needlessly, I opposed becoming a Christian. One day that would remarkably change when I turned to the Lord. In the world it was a time etched in history well-known for drugs, sex, and rock and roll. But on the flip side, the Jesus movement was well underway, and lives were being transformed. It was just a matter of time before that powerful movement would impact my life and the lives others, and then we would become Christ followers. Still to this day, lives are being touched and transformed, even as you read.

There was a silver lining in all of the above. When I finally stopped running from the Lord (and doing my own thing), my life was forever changed for the best. Not only was that good news, but some of the girls who conspired against me in the past eventually went on to become Christ followers too. Plus, we left the drug culture behind and all that goes with it, and instead, we traveled to outdoor Christian festivals. The festivals were like attending Woodstock, only with an entirely different scene, as they were full of thousands of youth praising the Lord through Christian contemporary music and more. That brings me to this verse in 2 Timothy 2:19: "Nevertheless the solid foundation of God stands, having this seal: 'The Lord knows those who are His,' and, 'Let everyone who names the name of Christ depart from iniquity.'" You see, the Lord had a bigger plan than me. He included some of them. He knows those who are His, and I would have never dreamt that one up.

IN CONCLUSION

On that potentially fatal day when the teens arrived with a knife, the outcome could have been grave. Yet I cannot but stop and think that it was the hand of God intervening in my life—a prodigal. He knew me before I was born, could see all the twists and turns that life would bring, and called me out of a dark pit. His plan for my life was and is better than any plan I could ever formulate. This is not just true for me but for anyone. He saw the rebel, but He looked beyond that, beyond my outward appearance, and into my heart. Then, the Lord took away my stony heart and gave me a new one—a heart after Him and His ways. Just like it says in Ezekiel 36:26 (Good News Bible), "I will give you a new heart and a new mind. I will take away your stubborn heart of stone and give you an obedient heart." Not only did the Lord protect me as in that intense crisis, but He did it again and again. God's sovereign plan not only covers my life but yours as well.

> O Lord, You have searched me and known me. You know my sitting down and my rising up; You understand my thought afar off. You comprehend my path and my lying down, and are acquainted with all my ways. For there is not a word on my tongue, but behold, O Lord, You know it altogether. You have hedged me behind and before, and laid Your hand upon me. ... For you formed my inward

parts; You covered me in my mother's womb. ... Your eyes saw my substance, being yet unformed. And in Your book, they all were written, the days fashioned for me, when as yet there were none of them.

— Psalms 139:1–5, 13, 16

CHAPTER 8

BULLIED IN THE BASEMENT: RAPE AND DRUGS IN SENIOR HIGH

Forgiveness is an act of the will, and the will can function
regardless of the temperature of the heart.

— Corrie ten Boom

Bullying in sexual assault involves the use of physical power, verbal threats, intimidation, manipulation, and control. It's all present in this chapter, and that is exactly what happened to me. The attributes of sexual assault fall under the guise of not only physical bullying but psychological violence. Therefore, it becomes a gender power play. Here, a power play is inflicted on an individual: me. The discrepancy over our size created an immediate imbalance between us—that of physical power combined with antisocial behavior, a crime of rape. Drug abuse can exacerbate aggressive character traits in an abuser. The above description parallels a son, but the son emulates his dad. The father and son duo took advantage of my naivety and trust, not just physically by the son but also emotionally due to the fact that at sixteen I was no match for grown adult men. And, unlike customs and cultures here in America, these people had emigrated from the Middle East ready to start a new life in the United States. What would I really know about immigration as a teen in the seventies? That subject was rarely mentioned in high school back then, unlike today, either way good or bad, it's become a national topic of discussion. Plus, I must add that immigration is not the point of this story.

It all started out rather innocently, or so it seemed. What did I know about boundaries and warning signs in relationships? Boundaries, warning signs, and red flags were not clearly taught like they are today. Again, there were no books to read about physical bullying, such as rape. The topic wasn't discussed in my school curriculum, inside my church, or on television, and furthermore, nobody openly talked about rape prevention or what to do if you are caught in such a catastrophic situation. There was no internet to research or to investigate life's dilemmas for helpful solutions. Now, we can access information by the tap of our finger on a screen. We're a planet in progress, thank God. What has been written or openly shared in this era, had it been uncovered yesteryear, could have possibly saved more lives from the ordeal of sexual abuse, harassment, and blatant, sinful acts. We would have (speaking for others like me) been empowered with tools to use or people to consult with had they existed. I may have experienced less pain and been better equipped with information to protect myself or turn to had it been in circulation. At sixteen, my innocence and naivety were exploited because of a lack of knowledge. There was no sweet sixteen.

In looking back, I wish *I would have never gone into the basement.* It would have spared me this chapter, but I am silent no more.

THE NEW KID ON THE BLOCK

Omar was a new senior and a bit older and I was a junior when we were introduced to each other in high school. He possessed a sly sense of charisma as the new kid on the block at school. Everyone noticed him. He was kind of cute and stood out from the others, as I had never seen a foreigner from the Middle East. He smoked pot along with other types of drugs, and that in itself made us fast friends. Most of the guys in school had better availability to drugs; even Omar knew where to go to get them. We were friends during a time when I wasn't following the Lord.

One day after school Omar brought me to his house to meet his family. When I met his father, he was quite charming and showed an interest in me. In hindsight, I wonder if that was a setup or just common courtesy. How would I know? Was he a manipulator? How could I tell? He was cordial, and I was polite upon introduction. The father was much my senior, appearing to be somewhere in his fifties. To me, that's all there was to it. I met Omar's dad and thought, *So what. Hurry up and get the intros over with so we can get out of here."* Back then, I was taught to respect and listen to adults, as well as always use my manners. Either way, then or now, caution must be exercised because not all motives are pure when meeting someone, even when good manners are used. Yet I wasn't thinking about wrongful intentions, considering a setup taking place in the near future, or picking up on signs of one ensuing.

Today, knowledge has truly increased, just like the Bible said it would be in the last days, so awareness has increased as well. I wish I had that surplus of insight back then. Although it's spread all over the internet today, back then, as you can see, the information highway was subpar. Even now, more home and school discussions need to transpire, so children and young adults know how to spot any deceptive plans lurking behind the impure motives of others. This is not to induce fear but to be prepared and aware in the event of a tragic situation because the world we live in is constantly changing.

Unfortunately, statistics on sexual abuse are highest in single-parent homes. Stats show an increase of youth being abused, mostly female, compared to statistics with both biological parents living in the home. After my parents' divorce, I chose to live with my mother. In coming from a nontraditional household, I was soon to become part of the first statistic. Nowadays, people are being armed with knowledge and insight on how to handle this national crisis concerning sexual abuse and human trafficking. More than ever, people are coming forward with their stories. I just wish we had been this vocal decades ago. As you can read today, the silence has been broken for good everywhere.

In regard to Omar, we were friends and only friends. He was a bad friend choice for me, but I didn't see it coming, and I was completely deceived. To me, his culture was fascinating. Their entire family emigrated here on business from the Middle East. He had a different culture, a unique dialect, and a dissimilar standard of living, and all of it intrigued me. I, on the other hand, lacked insight into their lifestyle, traditions, and practices. It was at Omar's house that I became fare game to the men, remaining completely unaware of what was happening.

On the day I went to Omar's house to meet his family, and totally unrelated to meeting them, I was in need of money to purchase new contact lenses. I rambled on to Omar who must have mentioned that need to his father upon my leaving. When I returned to visit on another day, his father entered the room and drew me aside privately, asking, "I heard you need money for your contact lenses. I would like to pay for them. How much money do you need?"

As I remember the conversation, his father seemed to be all ears. At the time, I didn't have money for contact lenses, and neither did my single mother. Omar's father offered to pay for them and insisted that I take his money. Right then, I thought, *Wow, how nice. That's awfully generous of him. He really doesn't have to do this, but I sure can use the money.* But *years* later as I reflected back, I realized that he could have asked to be repaid. He could have asked me for a payment plan. Yet nothing was asked of me. There were no strings attached to his giving. It was only after the money was spent that his agenda manifested. The father wasn't giving; he was baiting me. And how could I have known?

At sixteen, it never entered my mind that I was being baited, so I reasoned, *How can I go wrong? What a giving man. I was in need, and Omar's father met my need to buy contacts.* How could I have known that decision was going to turn into a power play coming back to haunt me?

Additionally, I never told my mom. I never said, "Some guy's dad just offered to buy me contacts."

My mom would have gone off and retorted, "Oh, no you don't. You don't want to do that! Give Omar's dad the money back." And she was not the type to explain her reasoning either. It would have been more like, "Just do what I'm telling you to do."

Instead, I told myself, *Why should I tell her? After all I need them, and there's the money.* I didn't think much outside of, *What a nice offer and just in time. This father must have money to spare, or he wouldn't be giving it to me when he has a family and a wife. Now, the need to see is met. No big deal.*

THE MANY FACES OF A BULLY, ABUSE, AND ADDICTION ◆ 119

NO BIG DEAL, OR SO I THOUGHT

After my purchase for corrective lenses, Omar's father came right out and asked me for sex in return for my new eyewear. Now he hit the bull's-eye: me. Herein lays the twisted mind, the indecent proposal, the further manipulation, and the exploitation of a minor. Need I say more? Even though I was rebellious, I was still stunned and shocked. How evil. That was overt sexual harassment, but it did not have a name. The term *sexual harassment* ended up in print much later. So there I stood in front of the father completely shaken, somewhat bewildered, and caught off guard by his tactics, the bait-and-switch kind.

His new behavior left me feeling quite uneasy. To top it off, as he was talking, he was practically backing me into the corner of the room. I did end up in the corner as I tried to edge myself away from his overbearing posture looming above me, causing me to look up at him. Certainly, I was oblivious to some of the distorted games people play. The Fathers new news left me wondering, *What am I going to do? I don't have any money. How am I gonna get out of this one?* At the same time, I thought, *Some dad is asking me for sex when I'm with his son. How sick. Just the thought of sex with someone's dad makes me want to puke.* The little girl in me felt queasy and undone, frozen in that moment. Suddenly, I was in fight-or-flight inside my head, fighting thoughts of real words being pushed upon me. I abhorred what was being said, but I was stifled, freezing in silence instead.

Here was another father figure who had violated my senses. That was bait and switch at its worst both times. As an adult, my friend's father was a sexual predator. I had been there before, years ago as a child with my best girlfriend's father. It's beyond sad that has happened twice. The first time, I was taken on a surprise birthday trip out of state. However, the second time, Omar's mom was upstairs during the discussion. I find the whole thing bizarre because the father didn't seem to care who was there. This prompted me to think, *Did she overhear us? Would she intervene? Would she condemn his behavior? What are their customs? I'm not sure.* I didn't know the answers. I was so young. But what I did know was that it felt awfully weird and didn't feel right. I didn't feel safe and knew I needed to get out of there fast. Those were the thoughts that began to surface in my frozenness. So to dodge the crisis in front of me, I actually got out of the house with some made-up, hurried up excuse. Afterward, I quit going to Omar's house to avoid a possible second confrontation over money and avoid being solicited for sex as payment for my contacts. I had no money to pay the father back after buying contacts, and he was not about to get his money after saying such things to me in private. The money, even if I did have the cash, was not to repay him, especially after he propositioned me for sex. It seemed that was my only plan within reach at the time. That was my rationale at sixteen. I did not understand right at that precise moment that he was manipulating the circumstances for his advantage. All I knew was that I had better stay away from the dad any way I could.

I didn't know I should tell someone. I didn't even think to tell my mom. As a backslidden addict, I just knew I'd gotten out of a dilemma. Plus, I didn't know I could have told the authorities. But who would they have defended? That is an entirely different subject. I'm guessing it would have ended up being a battle of he said, she said. And that too I wouldn't have known. All because I didn't understand what could happen to unaware and unprepared young girls. That's why I never said anything about the experience for years. The internet has exponentially expanded knowledge worldwide. And, if there had been a World Wide Web, I certainly would have looked into it further and then had a better plan.

Deep down, I knew had I not been friends with Omar, none of it would have happened. What brought us together as friends? Drugs masked in a cloak of deception. If I had been serving the Lord, I know I would have never been hanging out with him as I did. The Lord had and has a better plan for my life—our lives. His thoughts toward us and for us are better than any of our own thoughts. And one day I would come to realize this verse found in Isaiah 55:8–9: "'For My thoughts are not your thoughts, nor are your ways My ways,' says the Lord. 'For as the heavens are higher than the earth, so are My ways higher than your ways, and My thoughts than your thoughts.'" When we embrace the Word, we can replace our old patterns of thinking with scriptures that will renew our mind and our thought lives. We can overcome.

Furthermore, I must confess that scenario happened to me twice within one school year. And who wants to write about this? Still, I am silent no more. First, I was asked for sex by my friend's dad, a businessman. The second time I was propositioned by my art teacher while in the school building, which I did open up about in another chapter. His goal was sex in exchange for drugs, and that led to my goal, which was to stay away from him. Not only was the teacher being immoral, but I was totally appalled by such a suggestion coming from either adult.

After I became a Christian, I read in Mark 7:21–23: "For from within, out of the heart of men, proceed evil thoughts, adulteries, fornications, murders, thefts, covetousness, wickedness, deceit, lewdness, an evil eye, blasphemy, pride, foolishness. All these evil things come from within and defile a man." So until someone gives his or her life to the Lord, whereby that person's heart is changed, motives are changed, and intentions are transformed, we may be faced with the opposite of good: evil.

Honestly, I was faced with the reality of the above scripture on more than one occasion in an academic year. Here again, I was psychologically unprepared on how to handle a dilemma with older adult men interfering in my personal space. Both situations are despicable. Both are shocking to my ears to hear. And (thankfully) I managed to avoid those two men, a father and a teacher. How incredulous, revolting, and immoral. As a teenager, I buried those experiences down deep inside and didn't tell a soul, not even my mom.

When I was older, Mom did share with me something that she *never* told anyone herself. I'm not even sure if she told her own mother because that's how it was way back then, but one day she finally told me her story. She was raped after getting off the bus on her ride home after school. On that tragic day, as a teenager herself, she was walking home after being dropped off. It was a long walk for her, and there were undeveloped fields on both sides of the street. It was then she said, "Someone I didn't know grabbed me from behind and dragged me into one of the adjacent fields and raped me ..."

I brought this story up because my heart goes out to all the children, young girls, and women who have endured the unthinkable and never once were able to share what happened to them. Their stories have not been told. However, the Lord wants to heal those memories of untold stories. He can give us new memories and new stories to share, and He can restore our innocence. There is an answer for a brighter future ahead of us. It is knowing Jesus Christ.

Back then, I could have told my mom the events of the year, as she often told me, "You can always tell me anything," but I chose to numb myself instead and thought, *Why try.* It is nice to know I could have opened up, but I never said a word until years later when I was sober. Of course, it was due to the fact that drugs and money were involved, and I didn't want to go there. See where this can lead you when you're involved in a drug culture? I needed help, but I forwent the help (even from my mother) to squander my life on an addiction instead. I allowed the drugs to play with my head and numb my pain. You know what the hardest part is to admit? I wouldn't have believed anyone even if they did come and tell me that I was an addict. I am certain that I was totally and unjustifiably in denial of my own addiction and a few other things—sad but true.

On the other hand, if I did know I should have told someone, who could I tell that adult males were pursuing me, outside of my mother? How would I know if I could tell someone and that person would help? Who would that person believe, me or the professionals? Why would anyone believe an addict if I did tell on the men? And what if that became a power play of words, cover-up statements, and deception? Being realistic, that type of injustice did happen in the past, yet it still occurs in the here and now. However, the question remains: Would the sexual predators have said the truth or covered it up with a trail of lies? That too continues today. It would have been my word against their word. At sixteen, I had no voice, no formidable words, and no money to fight in court, and I felt I had no power to stand my ground against a businessman and a teacher. No protocol or information existed to guide, support, or protect me in that situation, unlike today.

Besides being young, how could I press charges on sexual harassment of a minor? Would sexual harassment have counted as an illegal offense? No. The real truth was that harassment grievance procedures were just being formulated in the seventies, and those procedures remained unestablished in many school systems, including mine. In looking back, it would have been another legal can of worms had I called those two men out as perpetrators. But there again, I wasn't thinking in regard to the legal system. I was trying to survive high school. Progress has advanced, and now we can yell and tell and turn to the right people. Status does not equal trust. Today's legal reforms, platforms, and social networks have brought this to the forefront. It's not new news anymore. Legal advice and education are now available for all to pursue. Sexual harassment *is* a form of bullying.

DRUGS AND MORE

In spite of the above, Omar and I continued to be friends, and we lived not too far from each other in the suburbs. So when I say the following, it's a known fact that drugs have no boundaries, whether you live in the inner city, the suburbs, or rural communities. Drugs do cross countries, cross borders, and cross backyards. Where I lived in the suburbs, Omar was the first person to offer me heroin. It's a huge epidemic today, but it's not a new one. It wasn't a new epidemic in the seventies either, yet it was growing among urban dwellers. The proliferation of heroin was not broadcast nationally, unlike today when it's talked about everywhere you go.

In spite of it all, I did not see the big question coming my way. And that conversation happened one evening while four of us were sitting in the car heading toward a Pink Floyd concert. All of a sudden, the question was popped: "Hey, do you want to try some heroin?"

At that point, all I could think was, *What, shoot up?* Unequivocally, I said no but hesitated for a few minutes before answering to the cajoling to try some. Thank God for my family bringing me up to know the Lord, taking me to church, and sharing with me David Wilkerson's graphic book on heroin. I never forgot any of it, as those pictures resurfaced in my head. That knowledge saved my life. Even in my rebellion, I could say no. All I remember at that moment in time is somewhere I was told, "It only takes one hit, and you'll be hooked on heroin." Then, the drug enslaves your mind, your body, and your future success. It will ruin your health. Heroin can kill you. Now, its carfentanil that will kill you. Yet, while in the car, I kept thinking, *If I do try it, what if I can't stop?* So for all those reasons, I said no when it came to heroin that night. At that point, I had a healthy dose of fear that the experience would yield an outcome I didn't want, namely, to become a slave to the bully heroin.

By the way, I'm not sure who the driver was that night taking us to the concert. He was a total stranger. Equally, I'm not sure if he had been shooting up heroin prior to picking me up, but I'm lucky to be alive considering that scenario has killed countless other lives. But elsewhere, in other cars on different nights, I witnessed my high school friends drink, do drugs, and drive, only to never drive again.

Toward the end of the school year, fantastic changes began to take place in my life, and I quit doing drugs altogether. I totally stopped cold turkey. As a prodigal, I rededicated my life to the Lord, and everything was changing for the best. Briefly, I did backslide, regress, and relapse. That was my biggest regret ever. After school was out for the summer, there was one final meeting with Omar. Deliberately, I stayed away from him for my own good.

However, when I became upset (and completely stressed out), I returned to an old behavior pattern, which was to get high. I also knew where to find quality hash when I wanted some. So late one night, I did a dumb thing without thinking of the consequences and without thinking I might be in jeopardy. I didn't think. But my mind turned to an old habit of numbing my stress versus dealing with it and learning new ways to handle it. Or, better yet, learning to turn to the Lord in prayer and ask Him for help. One of my favorite verses is Psalms 46:1–2, "God is our refuge and strength, a very present help in trouble. Therefore, we will not fear, even though the earth be removed." Until I learned to turn to the Lord for everything and study His word and know His voice, I made and still make mistakes like most people. Some were bigger than others, and here was one of those colossal mistakes.

On that particular night, I was feeling rather weak in the knees as my girlfriend coaxed me back to his house to get high, and I was the designated driver that night. At the time, we were both recovering drug addicts and new Christians. Going to Omar's house was going to be an enormous mistake—one I would regret for years. Had I refrained from going over, had I not listened to my friend beguile me, had I not listened to my head begging me for drugs, the outcome would have been much different. In the future, I needed inner healing from going over to visit. But most of all, I learned that nothing is too hard for the Lord, even our massive messes. It was the mistake of a lifetime, yet He healed me. "He heals the brokenhearted and binds up their wounds" (Ps. 147:3).

At first there was a small group of us getting stoned in his parents' basement on that tragic evening. And incidentally, that wasn't the only

THE MANY FACES OF A BULLY, ABUSE, AND ADDICTION ◆ 125

parents' basement available to get high in back in the day or to attend a party—both sad but true. By the end of the night, there were just the two of us, Omar and me. My girlfriend left with some friends in their car to go somewhere, and I was left behind. It was after hours, and I didn't care much about my curfew. Being a bit of a rebel (again), I didn't go home when I should have. I didn't care to go home stoned. Omar's parents were already upstairs in bed supposedly sleeping, and the house grew quiet with everyone gone. That's when he offered me some more dope—laced with what, I do not know—but we got high some more. And by then, I was blitzed but not passed out. I was fully aware and still coherent when, all of a sudden, Omar changed.

That's when it happened, after the binging; he turned around and pinned me to the couch in the basement. At the time, I wasn't so stoned that I didn't know what was going on. I did know it was truly *no* hallucination. I was also keenly aware of his father upstairs asleep or not. Perhaps, most of all, I was afraid his father would show up in the basement too. All at once, I felt sober minded, like a huge adrenalin rush hit me. My cortisol levels must have shot through the roof. My thoughts raced before me. *Do I scream? But who would come down the stairs? His father?* That concern was my greatest apprehension. For that reason, I did not yell, I did not scream, but I fought for freedom instead. *His dad is larger, and he's already asked me for sex.* That thought alone was paralyzing. *I'm afraid of two men in the basement. … What if his mother is fast asleep, and Omar's dad is not? What if his dad comes in the basement and locks the door?* The what-ifs continued to plague my mind, as I frantically wanted out of the basement somehow.

Struggling against Omar's weight, my tiny frame of 105 pounds or so was no match for his size and strength. I know I'm not the only one who has gone through a harrowing experience such as what went on that night. There are several references depicting such acts in the Bible that mention sexual assault. For instance, in 2 Samuel 13, there was a young woman named Tamar who was caught in a similar gruesome circumstance. She was sent over to Amnon's house to cook for him, and he had ulterior motives for her right from the start. In verses 11–12 and 14 of the Good News Bible, it reads: "As she offered them (the cakes) to him, he grabbed her and said, 'Come to bed with me!' 'NO,' she said. 'Don't force me to do such a degrading thing! That's awful!' But he would not listen to her; and since he was stronger than she was he overpowered her and raped her."

All because of his father upstairs, I was too afraid to scream out loud. Fighting with the perpetrator didn't help, but I tried. Due to the son and my size, I become not his opponent but his prey. I tried to stop him, but I knew not to scream. I was afraid of two men while I kept saying, "No, no, no. You can't do this," just like Tamar said in the Bible. During those terrifying moments in the basement, which I have omitted from this story, I was more terrified of what might happen if his dad did come downstairs to join him. Again, the what-ifs plagued my thoughts. *What if I am raped by his dad like I'm being raped right now?* That reality hung over my head as I tried to stand my ground. I was in grave trouble, realizing what was at stake, hoping it wouldn't come true, and at the same time trying to get away. It was there that I was sexually assaulted and bullied in the basement against my will, my protests, and my fighting.

ANOTHER TIME

With those memories running through my brain, I was reminded of another time that I did get away from a potential rape by some football players—Not just one but many. I never talked about it, and I didn't know that it had happened to others until one day I saw it plastered on television on the nightly news. When I was fifteen, there was a boy I liked very much. He was one of the cutest upperclassmen I ever did see, but I later found out the feelings weren't mutual.

Anthony lived a few streets from my house. When I dropped by and paid him a visit, we went into his family's basement to talk. (That visit took place way before Omar moved into the area.) That's when I found out he had company, all guys. Plus, Anthony's parents were out of town. That bit of added news on top of the guys being there made me feel somewhat uneasy and uncomfortable. Over time, I've learned to go with my gut feelings, but not on that day. I ended up going with what I actually heard.

After Anthony introduced me to his friends, all appeared well until I needed to use the bathroom. While I was in the bathroom, I overheard a loud discussion. It was all my virgin ears needed to hear (and yes, I was still a virgin). Whether they could or would carry out their intentions, I will never know. Upon leaving the bathroom, I made up a quick excuse and couldn't get out of there fast enough. Their lewd group discussion was to take turns raping me while the others watched. Right away, that topic obliterated my crush with the cute football player forever. His motives and intentions proved to be impure and disrespectful, to say the least. Needless to say, I am grateful that I escaped on that day too. In my lack of foresight, I never dreamt stuff like that went on in my backyard, in high schools, or on college campuses. Nobody talked about it. We are now sharing our real-life stories.

However, there were no words to describe rape by a person you knew back then. It didn't exist. People were not always believed, which is sad. It wasn't until *Ms. Magazine* published an article titled "Date Rape: A Campus Epidemic?" in 1982. It was Mary Koss who conducted a nationwide study on rape in the United States. She received credit for using the words *date rape* and *acquaintance rape*. She investigated students and compiled alarming evidence that justified her study and substantiated the new terminology. All of the above validated the violent acts against women. Her research and the article would give date rape and acquaintance rape credence.

Now, nothing is hidden from the public any longer. But for me in the seventies, it wasn't on any public forum as it is today. Mary Koss and others have paved the way and opened the door for women to site the violence of rape wrought against them, and their research helped to bring significant universal change. Since that time, other major movements have sprung forth to carry on the platform of change.

THE ER VISIT AND MY COVERUP

On that fateful night when the sexual assault was over, I left the basement as fast as my feet could possibly run. After that evening, I never saw Omar again. Within a few days' time, he boarded a plane to return to his homeland in the Middle East. All I ever knew was that he left. Conscious of that and knowing he was gone, I felt he got away with murder. After he violated me, over the course of several days, I was in excruciating pain.

I could barely walk and could hardly get to work or summer school, as something was seriously wrong. My lower back hurt so much I struggled to stand at work. The intense pain and pressure were hard to ignore. The pain shot through my lower spine, radiating down into my toes. My range of motion had greatly diminished. At the time, I had fought for freedom. Then soon afterward, I became worried, concerned, and overwhelmed as I headed toward the ER.

Knowing I had been raped (as a teenager), I trusted no one right then. I also did not want to tell anyone I had been raped because I felt uncertain as to what would follow if I did say something. Therefore, I protected myself by remaining silent on that subject, while my dad took me to the hospital. My coverup story to him and the ER doctor became, "I fell down some steps and hurt my back during summer school." I decided it was best to stick with my story of falling down the stairs. In that hour, that sounded reasonable and believable. How could I have guessed that was a popular line to use? I would not have known that back then. After all, I was afraid to tell my father what really happened, and I was afraid to tell the doctor the truth as well. I was more afraid to tell my dad than to tell the doctor (and I never did tell my dad what happened).

Rather, I decided to avoid the truth at all costs by trying to minimize it. I felt embarrassed and unsure of the reaction of others to that sort of news, especially men. I felt it was best to avoid the conflict of explaining the what, when, where, why, and how the injury occurred. Nobody taught us in our mandatory sex education class how to handle that type of tragedy, especially if you knew the person. I never dreamt my no would be ignored. Resources weren't assessable. There was no hotline to call or crisis center to visit, most unlike today. Yet, in the seventies, a few changes were beginning to take place, and they varied from state to state. When it came to the doctor privately questioning my story, I stubbornly held onto my version, dodging the truth and sticking with my faulty facade.

Upon examination, the doctor informed me of what was going on with my female anatomy. The misalignment was the cause of the acute pain on my lower spine. Even though I was fully aware as to what had taken place, I chose to bite my tongue while he explained the results of my exam. Many questions ensued, but after a few minutes, the doctor quit pressuring me. With my dad waiting in the next room, I thought, *How can I talk about this? Do you think I'm going to volunteer what happened to me and bring on more of a problem? Make it even bigger? No, it's better to keep quiet, to lay low, and to play stupid.* The truth was I felt afraid, unsure, intimidated, and unprepared for a male inquisition right then and even later. Furthermore, I was unwilling to become unguarded and unprotected in that situation to more men on a sensitive subject in a court of law or to press charges on a person living in a different country, vulnerable to an extensive and expensive process, for which there was no money. What if Omar returned, and he and his father came in and said the opposite, turning it into another he-said, she-said battleground? I wasn't ready for any of it. The culmination of those thoughts led to why I remained silent as a teenager right then and later. Besides, the rapist was gone. He had left the country. So for years, I kept my mouth shut until the doors for healing and restoration opened up.

I later discovered through online research that rape kits were just being created in the late seventies, and DNA testing didn't exist until the late eighties. So none of that was available as a tool to help me. At sixteen, I thought I had made the right decision to not say a word. It was to spare myself more emotional distress. Inwardly, I refused to subject myself to anyone or anything else involved with that situation. Trust was shattered. I do know today that I'm not the only one who made that choice a long time ago due to lack of resources and the unrelenting candor needed. Besides that, you were up against a shortened statute of limitation in reference to a crime such as rape.

By the end of my appointment, the doctor excused me from work and prescribed bed rest, medication, and physical therapy. Shortly thereafter, I was back to work and fresh out of summer school, graduating at seventeen and hiding my troubling secrets. But one day in the far-off future, all of that would indeed change because healing would come.

With all that being said, I turned to the Lord in my distress, and He heard my cry. Likewise, He didn't abandon me. He answered me. I am forever grateful for His love.

IN CONCLUSION

You might be thinking after having read this chapter that this is sexual assault, and I agree with you, but bullies also rape. They use physical control, fear, and manipulation to conquer their prey. An exhaustive list of the definition of a bully and bullying can be found in the introduction. Drugs are also a bully. Had I not been involved with drugs back then my circle of friends and acquaintances would have been entirely different, along with the memories. I was raped by an addict; both are bullies within a drug culture.

Had I not backslid to begin with and returned to my old ways, it's possible the entire scenario would have never occurred, but it did. After that sudden tragedy, I not only forgave the person and others along the way, but I returned to the Lord to continue my journey with Him. Instantaneously, I was delivered from drugs and never went back to that lifestyle ever again.

Using the Keys to Forgiveness Scale, that life event quantifies a ten, which means it was hard to endure, extremely difficult to walk through, and challenging to forgive and get over. It took a large amount of time, grace, and continued forgiveness as I overcame those memories and let go. The day arrived when I needed help. That's because I grew tired of appearing like everything was OK when it wasn't on top of looking at my hidden, secret pain. I could ignore and repress what happened for only so long, and one day help became available. With that purpose-driven invitation, I seized the day. To me, it was the Lord providing a way out from it all. When those opportunities finally arrived, it was because more Christians began offering individual and group support for sexual assault victims. They recognized the need and set out to fill it. With that availability, I applied myself to overcome the past along with the Lord's mercy and grace. In the mix was the love of the Lord and the people He used in the process, all of which are mentioned in the "Strategies for Overcoming" section of this book. Those choices combined with inner healing from above led to my healing and restoration. Much of that happened years later after resources were developed and became accessible and the doors were opened for recovery and ministry. Again, I am forever grateful for a breakthrough in an area that has affected countless lives.

The Lord is our compassionate High Priest. "Seeing then that we have a great High Priest who has passed through the heavens, Jesus the Son of God, let us hold fast our confession. For we do not have a High Priest who cannot sympathize with our weaknesses, but was in all points tempted as we are, yet without sin. Let us therefore come boldly to the throne of grace, that we may obtain mercy and find grace to help in time of need" (Heb. 4:14–16).

If any of this has happened to you, there is a way out of your pain. The Lord wants to help you become whole and free again. He wants to reach in and heal your memories over something you had no control over, and He wants to wipe away your tears and restore your innocence.

> It is better to trust in the Lord than to put confidence in man.
>
> — Psalms 118:8

> Trust in the Lord with all your heart, and lean not on your own understanding; in all your ways acknowledge Him, and He shall direct your paths.
>
> — Proverbs 3:5–6

> They surrounded me like bees; they were quenched like a fire of thorns; for in the name of the Lord I will destroy them. You pushed me violently, that I might fall, but the Lord helped me.
>
> — Psalms 118:12–13

CHAPTER 9

MY COUSIN ON POLYS
(PLEASE QUIT—ANYONE—BEFORE YOU DIE)

God can bring peace to your past, purpose to your present,
and hope to your future.

—Tony Evans (@drtonyevans)

When I was young, I could never understand why my father kept us away
from his side of the family, and he came from a large family. However, that
meant I rarely saw my cousins to play with or to later hangout with, and
we were all close in age. Over time, I got it, and it was in our family's best
interest. My only wish is that the reason why we were kept separated could
have been explained to me because I always wondered why. On average,
our family must have seen my dad's side of the family once, maybe twice
a year, if that. It was just the way it was.

In my opinion, what wasn't explained to me was that when my dad
became a Christian, he stayed away from all of the family abuse (which
I won't get into here), the boozing, and the drugs that most of his side of
the family became enmeshed in. He stayed uninvolved in that lifestyle and
instead remained clean and sober and greatly involved in church.

On the flip side, his family stayed away from him and the Word of
God, which he tried to share with them on numerous occasions throughout
the years. They replied no to anything Dad tried to share. In other words,
he was rejected for being a Christian and for taking a stand on what was
right. Many times, he reached out to his own family, and many times they

replied no once more to accepting Jesus in their hearts and yes to more drugs and more alcohol. That in and of itself consumed many lives. My dad has outlived his entire family, including all of his siblings and nearly all of my cousins. Imagine that.

How was his life different from theirs? How did he escape it all? That information my dad did share with me. The reason was his grandmother, my great-grandmother, who I did get to visit as a child. She taught my dad about the Lord. She loved the Lord and impacted his life in a great way by sharing with my dad about Jesus while he was growing up, thereby planting good seeds inside his head and heart. And that bore fruit later in life, as he went on to serve the Lord.

Likewise, you can read in Matthew 13 a parable about a sower sowing seed. In verses 8–9, it says, "But others fell on good ground and yielded a crop; some a hundredfold, some sixty, some thirty. He who has ears to hear, let him hear!" On this note, may you and I continue to reach out to others and plant good seeds with the hopes of yielding a harvest one day. We may never know until we get to heaven how much we have touched others with the seeds we have sown into them.

MY COUSIN

On the other hand, with so many cousins in the family, my mom used to say, "Out of all the male cousins, Carl has all the looks." As a teenager, I agreed that he was the best looking of them all. My girlfriends would say, "Too bad he's just your cousin." But they could date him, and I would not. That was then and this is now. Carl is gone. However, it didn't start out that way. It ended that way.

His extensive drug abuse combined with some serious alcohol intake evolved over time. He just about blew his brains out as a habitual addict and alcoholic. Eventually, his looks waned, his strength evaporated, and his organs began to fail as he grew older. In the future, he was in need of both a kidney and liver transplant in order to survive. In time, Carl lost everything he ever owned or worked for, including his business, his home, and his vehicle. That was because his drug-dependent lifestyle was killing him. In the end, he was unable to work or to find work or to even hold down a job as time ticked by.

By the time I found Carl as an adult (he moved around a lot), he was extremely gaunt and in poor health. He lived in a rundown halfway house on some shady, dimly lit side street, located in a part of town where I would never want to go or live, not in a million years. Later on, I did find *bravery* to make the trek to visit, but only after telling someone where I was going and taking a friend. At that point in time, flip phones were in use, and they were not that smart in finding you if you needed to be tracked down. They did not track your every move like the smartphones of today. Plus, there wasn't a camera or recording device built inside the phone to capture live events if needed, and you had to tap each key to text, which highly frustrated me. Nowadays, it's much faster to voice activate a text. In the past, you needed to inform someone of your whereabouts for your own protection, especially if you were a female, and that's definitely an important side note that still exists today. Putting all of that aside, I made the trip and paid my cousin a visit.

By grace, I braved the elements in that part of town, going into places I normally wouldn't go in, so I could tell my cousin once more about a loving savior, Jesus Christ. It was just like my father did all those years before, as he tried to reach out to his own family members. This reminds me of a verse in 1 Corinthians 3:6–7. "I planted, Apollos watered, but God gave the increase. So then neither he who plants is anything, nor he who waters, but God who gives the increase." I don't know how the journey truly ended in those last moments for my cousin when that day arrived (although I can only imagine), except I do know seeds were planted inside his mind, soul, and heart to know the Lord—not just in the past but on that particular day and shortly thereafter.

A few months later, my dad and I followed up, and we brought Carl into our family for one final Christmas. When we entered the shelter where he was staying, it was cold, quiet, and dreary as we tried to locate him for the trip. There was no one to greet us upon entering the building, but a passerby knew Carl and went to get him while we waited. The surroundings did not emulate Christmas. There were no stockings hanging by a tree in the foyer because there was no Christmas tree.

There were no visible signs of any holiday, just a musty, stagnant odor lingering overhead. That smell made me want to hold my breath, but I couldn't as we waited. I wanted to wait outside but didn't. Of course, I never would admit that to anyone, except for just now. Honestly, I was a bit creeped out by everything around me, while we both stood and waited for Carl to come downstairs, as we were not permitted upstairs. Sometimes that is where drugs will take you—into places you don't want to visit or live. We went inside to get him anyway, and more grace came. Only that time, I was glad my dad and I went together to pick him up. The conditions took bravery (once again), while everything around me cried, "Get out!"

On that particular Christmas, when we finally arrived at our destination, everyone reached out and shared more than food, laughter, and games. We set out to share the warmth of family, make new memories, and demonstrate God's love. What if that was to be Carl's last Christmas? Then what I really wanted him to know one last time would be God's love for him.

YOU ARE CHASING YOURSELF INTO AN EARLY GRAVE

How did Carl get that way? Well, Carl started doing drugs and drinking in his teens. Then he never quit. He said, "I quit," at times, but in the end, time told another truth, which was he never quit abusing drugs or alcohol. If Carl were alive today, he would be in his sixties. That's a lot of stuff over the years in his head. He couldn't stay away from drugs and alcohol as a polydrug abuser. Bullied by drugs most of his life as a polydrug addict, it appeared that he could not say no.

Polydrug abuse is when a person abuses multiple substances in many combinations, which are lethal when used together. At any time, polysubstance abuse can lead to seizures, strokes, respiratory failure, hypoxic brain damage, dementia, Alzheimer's, and sudden cardiac arrest. Some of those conditions affected not only Carl but other family members who lost their battles with addiction. Research has indicated those quantitative facts are being underreported by family, friends, and the medical profession alike. So I want to talk about it from an up-close, personal point of view. To me, if one life can be spared or saved, then this write was worth it.

Back in the day, as I have said above, I rarely saw my cousins, but when I did, we all partied behind our parents' backs before I became a Christian. That is probably another sound reason as to why we were kept apart, which was to avoid every toxic influence while we were growing up. Because from time to time when my cousins could finally drive, I would end up sharing a joint or other things with them as a rebellious teen and nonbeliever, knowing all too well they were able to get their hands on stronger stuff to feed my habit. I am truly blessed and grateful that I gave it all up and lived. I didn't stay stuck in it for years; I got out of it forever.

Overall, the biggest difference between Carl and me, or my cousins and me, was that I walked away from it all and stayed away from it all, just like my father. My dad never became involved with any addiction, and I walked away from the bully drugs. I owe that to my Christian upbringing (along with all the seeds that were planted inside of me) in addition to asking Jesus to be Lord of my life. For me, life went on, and I stayed away from temptation, meaning I stayed away from drugs. I wanted no part of that lifestyle or culture, having been ensnared by it myself, once I got out of it for good. For Carl, he ended up at death's door refusing to change and refusing help.

My auntie, Carl's mother, died an alcoholic too. Ravaged by alcoholism, she bled to death inside a hospital. The prognosis in the end was that nothing more could be done to save her. I rarely, if ever, saw her except in the end lying in a casket. When I heard about the funeral, I asked her grown son, my cousin, if I could speak at her funeral. By then, my father's legacy of sharing Christ with his family inspired me to do the same in that hour of opportunity. I also knew that my dad did not like to speak in front of large crowds. Not that I liked it any better, but I decided that I would be happy to take the place of my father and speak on his behalf. So it was there I took the liberty to share in my father's legacy of sharing Christ and His love that He has for each one of us. I also recited John 11:25: "Jesus said to her, 'I am the resurrection and the life. He who believes in Me, though he may die, he shall live.'" My burden that day included not only my aunt and extended family members but anyone who did not know the Lord—really, any person who had ears to hear about the love of Christ spoken of in John 3:16.

Finally, after the funeral when the family met together, I was pulled aside and verbally assaulted (bullied) by my dad's mother, the grandmother I barely knew and rarely saw, for sharing Christ to a crowd. But when I spoke at the funeral, there were others who spoke about Christ as well from the podium. So why she chose me that day, I'll never know. I can only guess. She suddenly became furious with me for telling the audience about Jesus, which caught me shockingly unprepared and off guard, but I didn't argue with her, and I'll tell you why. Although Grandma was entitled to her opinion, I had access to the opportunity to speak through the grandson of the deceased, my cousin, who was also the executor of everything. On top of that, I was next to a room full of relatives and acquaintances when she went off, and the last thing I wanted to do was argue over her issue in front of everyone. Certainly, her words hurt more than words could say, but in that moment, I decided to use some self-control and walk away. Yet, after our discussion, she never spoke to me again, and that was the last time I saw her alive. To this day, I hold no hard feelings toward her (and have long since forgiven her). I also have no regrets in trying to reach out and share the Gospel.

SOBER OR NOT?

After my aunt's funeral, my cousin returned to his home state to carry on with a life of drugs and drinking, and within a few short years, that's when it happened. Carl was binging on. … Well, I'm not sure what all he was binging on. They say any polydrug combination may be your last combination. It was that lethal cocktail that sequestered him inside of a hospital and then back to a halfway house, eventually leading to hospice care and his final breath.

Before that time arrived, my cousin and I would talk on the phone, and occasionally, Carl would say, "I am trying to stay sober," or, better yet, "I'm still not using." Additionally, I couldn't hold his hand in sobriety no matter what he said—truth or consequence. He lived far away, and he would have to do it himself and want to stay sober. I couldn't do it for him, even after numerous conversations. By then, we were more than grown adults—no more kid stuff. He was states away and responsible for his decisions, along with the outcome of those defining choices. I couldn't rescue him. Instead, I continued to pray and reach out to him when I felt prompted to call.

However, small talk and skirting the issue works for only so long, and then, "your sins will find you out," as the scripture says in Numbers 32:23. It was only later that Carl made his way to a family reunion for all eyes to see. Instead of sobriety like he had claimed, he and his friends arrived fully blitzed out of their gourds on a mixed cocktail of hardcore drugs. The extended family gathering of relatives, friends, and acquaintances couldn't help but stand and stare and wonder as they made a public spectacle of themselves for all eyes to see, and that's when the conversation became difficult.

My immediate family was not only surprised but devastated to see the effects of hardcore substance abuse after decades of using—not years but decades. Then the excuses began to fly, as my cousin tried to downplay his intoxication and lie about his habit in front of us. After some discourse and some acting-out behaviors by Carl and his friends (which I won't get into), they all stumbled off the premises to never come back again.

MY LAST CALL

Throughout the years, I have tried to stay in touch with Carl. Sometimes it appeared that no news was good news, as the saying goes, but that was not true toward the end with my cousin. By the time I received an update, he had already undergone a liver and kidney transplant. Unbelievably, he received both organs and was on the mend for a short season. Perhaps he wasn't using during that time, or in the hospital he must have completely dried out. Or maybe it was a combination of the two. Whatever the case, it didn't last; his willpower slowly diminished as he gave up and gave in again. Yet, due to the fact that Carl didn't maintain his sobriety upon his release and returned to his old ways, that choice led to a different outcome. The difference being that time ran out. He died in his addiction, which was troubling news in the end to know. Yet another family member had died in his addiction, and after I had reached out to him and encouraged him to stay sober and get help. But you try because you care about the person. Whether the person is a friend or family member, you love the addict, not the addiction. You want the person to be clean, to be sober, to know Christ, and to be alive and well.

Still, it was during one of his relapses that my cousin began calling me, and the stories ensued. First, I believed him and even helped him. Later, he needed money for a court case, then he needed money for a fine, then much later he needed money for a medical bill, or so he implied and pleaded. Carl was also fired from several jobs; he would later confess that to me as well. He couldn't seem to keep any sort of employment that came his way. During his relapse, he made many calls to me and to others asking for money, which led to my confronting his substance abuse and where it was taking him. I earnestly warned him, "Don't call and lie to me over the phone. I can hear it in your voice. You're stoned. It's going to kill you if you don't stop. Can't you see this? You're making no sense, and it's only noon! You are only calling here to get money for drugs and alcohol. I know where your money is going. Who can believe anything you say anymore? You're going to die if you don't quit." Carl admitted right then and there to using his money on street pills.

Amazingly, I could look the amount of his request up online to know the street value of his pills versus what he wanted for bills, and those figures matched. That type of knowledge at my fingertips had an immediate effect upon confronting my cousin. I couldn't have gathered that insight years earlier because it didn't exist. Besides, I had to address the situation; he was wasting my money and making up lies for more. Carl wasn't being honest, and I could tell he was using. He even laughed about it, and it's not a laughing matter. For him, the narcotics turned to heroin. The heroin turned to meth and alcohol because he informed me of that too. To top it off, who knows what else and in what combination went inside his head.

On my cousin's very last call, I earnestly asked him to get some help. "Are you checking in with anyone? Are you going to church anywhere? Do you still have a Bible? Please read your Bible. Will you go back to church? Why don't you go back to rehab?" I asked those questions because Carl actually did involve himself in church years prior, and he had been in rehab before. In those fleeting moments, I encouraged him the best I could to turn his life around, go back to church and turn to Christ, and ask Him to deliver you from your addiction. I knew firsthand that God can deliver a person from addiction.

Carl's answer was, "There's a church down the street, but I don't go. Sometimes I have the TV on in the background and listen to a pastor on TV." He also shared, "I'm on Medicaid, and I'm broke. I've had some kind of mini stroke and can't walk like I used to. I try to get it together, but it's been tough because I'm having seizures. I've been in and out of the hospital. The doctors started me on a new medication, and now my kidneys aren't working right. So I'm not doin' really good. And I can't get a job. It's been really hard. There's no money coming in to do a thing."

At that point, Carl could barely talk coherently, as I was trying to make sense of what he was saying. Was that the outcome of it all? Was he left mentally impaired, or was he drunk or high on something? His speech was slow and slurred. It may have been due to his addiction, as he was still using on top of everything else mixed together, or the seizures may have led to a speech impediment. I couldn't tell. But it appeared that my cousin's polydrug lifestyle took the best of him, destroying his brain cells and time.

That was the last time I spoke to Carl, as his phone was later turned off, and I had no other contacts to call. I didn't even have an address due to his many moves. Eventually, I learned he had entered hospice care and passed away of both substance abuse and kidney failure. The most difficult part to acknowledge, watch, hear, or write is this: his entire family died because of their addictions.

Life is worth living. Know that we each have a destiny, a purpose, and a future because of Christ.

IN CONCLUSION

I cannot make the end result of this story pretty, but the end result of addiction isn't always pretty either. I wanted to say great things. I wanted to write that it all worked out and my cousin's life had changed for the better, but I couldn't. In the end, my cousin was bullied to death by decades of drug abuse and alcoholism. It started out with him using weed as a teenager, which led to a lifetime of polysubstance abuse and eventually a physical death row. The culmination of his lifestyle had led to toxic brain injury and more. This type of brain injury produces memory loss, inability to concentrate, loss of motor skills, and seizures. It can progress to destruction of bodily systems, retardation, a vegetative state, and death. Alongside organ failure, his life was dramatically cut short. It didn't have to end that way, yet it did. The hardest part to know was that he briefly turned his life around with a will to get better, but he walked away from it all.

Carl loved the bottle and the drugs that have so many names. Once he boldly confessed to me, "I know it will either take prison, or I'm gonna die doin' what I want. That's the only way I see myself quitting drugs or drinking." With that startling confession, the latter came to pass. My cousin was bullied to death by living a polydrug lifestyle. The addiction was severe and beyond his willpower, meaning he didn't want to quit— not then, not yet, not even when help was provided. Although, the fact remains that without a lasting recovery period and total abstinence, drugs and alcohol stole his life. So once and for all, anyone, please quit before you die. There is a better life worth living. I will sum this up by adding that nothing is beyond the Lord's power to deliver, heal, and restore an individual. It's *never* too late to stop and start over.

> Then the righteous will answer Him, saying, "Lord, when did we see You hungry and feed You, or thirsty and give you drink? When did we see You a stranger and take You in, or naked and clothe You? Or when did we see You sick, or in prison, and come to You?" And the King will answer and say to them, "Assuredly, I say to you, inasmuch as you did it to one of the least of these My brethren, you did it to Me.
>
> — Matthew 25:37–40

> He brought them out of darkness and the shadow of death, and broke their chains in pieces. Oh, that men would give thanks to the Lord for His goodness, and for His wonderful works to the children of men!
>
> — Psalms 107:14–15

CHAPTER 10

FIT, THIN, AND BULLIED

Step into your purpose: Anytime you move away from where you used to be, somebody who knew you back then is going to make some kind of noise about it.

— T. D. Jakes

Take this journey with me. It is completely unlike the last chapter and purposefully so. And frankly, it is entirely different compared to everything else in this book.

So, after I became a dedicated Christian at seventeen, a friend of mine brought me to what I thought was a really cool vegetarian restaurant within a college community. Although today you may see a vegetarian or vegan food establishment everywhere you go, back then they were basically unheard of. Before I ventured into that type of restaurant, indeed there were french fries. When I was in high school, fast food and french fries were finally permitted in school lunches, and those munchies became all the rage. For a while, french fries were my lunch staple. However, after graduating, I visited the new vegetarian restaurant often, and their menu whet my appetite for more. Everything was delicious. After the initial taste test of a new menu entrée from the foodie palace, I would return home to try and make some of their most luscious recipes. That discovery, I believe, contributed to my wellness, especially compared to what I used to eat.

During high school and immediately after graduation, I had a diet rich in candy bars, Pepsi, and TV dinners, usually consumed on the go. And if there were no frozen dinners available, my favorite fast foods existed for me to gulp down instead. That routine led to the summer I put on ten pounds, enjoying the best peanut butter milkshakes I ever did taste. Those frosty delights were created from a local custard stand down the street. The thicker the shake, the better it tasted. The shakes were beyond scrumptious. They became addictive, and that's what I ate for lunch until I hopped on the scale. If I couldn't walk there, my car knew the way to the custard stand. Eventually, I broke the routine and tried to eat right. It was either break the routine or purchase more clothes in a larger size, and I really didn't want to shop for a different size.

Most likely, I would have never known back then that food equals health. I didn't give it any thought, and most people never talked about healthy food choices. Betty Crocker appeared to be the only way to cook. Everyone seemed to own a Betty Crocker cookbook. That new interest in health took me past my late teens (and Betty Crocker) clear through adulthood, amid a few food detours along the way, which flourished into eating clean and green in the end. In looking back, I know finding that special restaurant and making some changes helped me to get better after the drugs I had polluted my body with in high school, along with remaining drug free to this day. And I know that type of diet also helped me overcome a few problems in the future once I stuck with it. I credit the Lord for all of these things. He redeemed my life and changed me from the inside out, body, mind, and heart.

After years (and years) of eating instant, highly refined, and processed foods, which had been the norm for me to indulge in and savor, the diet continued until I did some research and embraced change little by little. Due to my inadequate food choices and lack of sticking to healthier alternatives, around the year 2002, I was diagnosed with prediabetes and given a prescription for a lifetime of medication. That was a result of improper food habits and out-of-control cravings, which I admit I succumbed too—not only then but years earlier when I ended up with reactive hypoglycemia. What a serious wake-up call that was to my ears, my head, and my health. However, the prediabetic condition completely disappeared when I rerouted my diet and abstained from those bad food habits. I had returned once again to eating clean and green like I tried to do from time to time, but I didn't stick with it until I became super determined. In fact, because of my major food overhaul, I never did fill the prescription, and the proof was in the test results. Even though it didn't happen overnight, the outcome made me a believer as I was gradually healed. Honestly, I know the right diet will help a former drug addict recover and those with other ailments feel better by strengthening the body and mind with nutrients to replenish what was lost, depleted, or damaged. On a practical level, aiming to eat right will help any individual go forward to recapture or keep his or her health, young or old.

Although most of this chapter is unrelated to drug addiction, the reality of restoring health during or after an illness, addiction, or trauma will bring strength, wellness, and healing as a result. The pursuit of health leads one to discover the truth behind the saying: You are what you eat. The goal of proper nutrition provides restorative capabilities by creating and assisting in maintaining a healthy body and mind. What could be wrong with that?

Yet herein lies the twist—a complete 180. Elsewhere in this book, I have cited examples when I have been bullied for being overweight. Now, I'll share some occurrences when I've been bullied for being thin. Who would think you could be bullied for being thin? I certainly would have never dreamt that one up or thought it could happen. To top it off, as I grew older, I assumed this bullying stuff would not survive the passing of time. I surmised that bullying shouldn't exist at all on any topic after a certain age, but this is not true. Just look at the media, for instance, or politics. Unfortunately, bullying exists in every socioeconomic and age group. Honestly, I'm amazed by the negative remarks people say to others instead of encouraging one another.

While I'm on the subject of diet leading to health, know it wasn't a quick fix like I mentioned. It evolved over years until it became a way of life. Besides that, I enjoy reading nutritional books and periodicals. I have read this type of genre on healthy eating for most of my life. I'm amazed by individuals who won't study health but like to bully me for trying to better myself. So let's demystify the idea that bullying has no age limit and acknowledge that every age has been bullied. Beyond this reality and dealing with it, forgiveness is a key to overcoming opposition.

In life, I take this scripture in 1 Corinthians 3:16 to heart. "Do you not know that you are the temple of God and that the Spirit of God dwells in you?" Add to this scripture an old quote that I mentioned earlier: You are what you eat. That would explain my philosophy in trying to take care of this temporary temple from a physical standpoint. It certainly has become a fundamental reason as to why I sought to correct the wrong food choices of the past, which actually led to illnesses in my future, either ignorantly, willfully, or because I had no choice in what was placed in front of me to eat while growing up in a fast-food culture. The goal became to change my health status. This scripture also applies: "My people are destroyed for lack of knowledge" (Hosea 4:6). Gaining knowledge gave me tools to improve the way I eat, so I could feel well as I aged. And most of all, it was because I grew tired of being sick and tired and not always knowing why or how to fix it.

BODY-SHAMING

Realistically, I can say that I've experienced both sides of the coin: bullied for being heavy and thin. Either way, they are both considered a form of body-shaming. And either way, I grew tired of hearing about my size.

In reference to my weight loss, I came up with an analogy to explain my situation. If you were to take my body, take off my head, and put on the head of a teenager, you would say, "You look great." If you again took off my head and put on the head of a college student, you might say once more, "You look great." But instead of a compliment for losing weight and, of course, keeping my head on my body today, I hear from time to time, "You need to put on some weight," or, "You need to eat more and put some meat on." These comments have come from people in my own age group. And then there are others who say quite the opposite: "You look great for your age. What's your secret?" Or, "You don't look your age. What are you doing different?" So where did the first perception come from? Now that I'm older, must I look a certain way?

In trying not to offend anyone, isn't this a preconceived opinion on how I or any person must look *after* a certain age? Wouldn't that opinion be stereotypically biased and based on what? Fact or fiction? It's kind of outdated and obsolete. Those opinions originated years ago and have been passed down for generations now. Still, they are based on what? In all honesty, I've worked to maintain my size after losing weight, and I have worked to keep it that way for years by eating right, staying active, and exercising, which you know wasn't always the case. And still, people find fault with me on the way I look to them. Having said this, I'll just keep my head on my body for now.

Right now, I weigh what I weighed in high school after putting on all the excess weight I gained when I went to college give or take a pound or so. And the weight I gained in college was due to indulging in their food court and eating as much as I wanted when I wanted, and I didn't care how many helpings I ate (well, at least not in the beginning). This reminded me of how I used to eat as a child until I caught myself. At that point, the cafeteria was like an endless buffet—until I gained twenty-nine pounds, to be exact, and my face broke out in massive zits. After that supersize experience and out-of-control acne, I turned things around with much self-discipline and lost the added weight by going back to eating healthy. I decided it was better to avoid the buffet style of eating as much as possible. The benefit was that within a month's time, my acne vanished, and I shed the excess weight. Perhaps I didn't lose all the weight that fast, but certainly the acne disappeared within thirty days of eating right, and I'll never forget it.

Much later, I gained weight again. Only that time, I put on twice as much weight with my second child as compared to my first, gaining roughly forty-six pounds. And once more, I had thrown dieting out the window. As you can read, I love to eat, and eating the wrong types of food just gets me into trouble. Eventually, I would ditch every food that piled on the pounds every time. It prompted me to make use of what I had previously learned, which led me back to eating clean and green. The only difference was that after my second child was born, someone said in passing, "You look so matronly." I was thirtyish at the time. Not only was I embarrassed and feeling rather guilty for gaining close to fifty pounds, but I was surprised by the blatant honesty. Or was it intentionally meant as an insult to body-shame me? Maybe it was my clothing choices, or possibly was it my appearance. I'm not sure which way they intended it to come across. Today, that type of comment is called mommy-shaming, which is another word in circulation used to discredit a mother who doesn't look perfect after giving birth or having children. The language used is not designed to encourage or to build another up; it's used to tear another down. We must learn to let it go and not take it to heart. Regardless, that person's statement didn't help back then regarding my postpartum look (and maybe this has happened to you too). Either way, forgiveness applied for sure. I wore a size 16 after giving birth, and no one really knew I was in a private battle to lose weight, as I suffered trying to shed the pounds. I couldn't shake off the baby weight no matter how hard I worked at it or sweat for it until I changed my diet.

Ironically, it appeared that whenever I returned to eating what I came to describe as my main diet, a whole-foods diet, it enabled me to lose the pregnancy weight I gained and couldn't get rid of for almost five years. That meant I returned to the weight I am today, which is the weight I was in high school, give or take a pound or so. I wear the same size now as I did back then, yet I feel healthier than I have ever felt in the past. If someone comes up to me and tells me I'm too thin, I realize they don't know what I went through to get healthy and stay that way. Prejudice based on size and age discrimination has seemingly crept into society, informing us how we *should* look as a mature adult. Don't settle for this fallacy on how we should look at a certain age.

Besides, on the advent of my second child, I chose once again to not eat as I usually do, eating everything and anything I wanted; after all, I was pregnant. Pregnant women are told they are eating for two, so I ate for two. It was certainly a surprise to me that while being older and pregnant, my body didn't work the way it had worked the first time, much to my disappointment. But also, the first time I ate only healthy foods and exercised. With my first child, I was back into prepregnancy clothes as soon as I had my baby and was out the door as soon as I could exercise again. Pregnant nine years later and undisciplined in my diet and exercise (meaning I sort of quit both and took a detour), I packed on the baby weight. I was shocked when I stood on the scale. Candidly, I thought, *As soon as I deliver this baby, I'll just bounce back to my usual size like I did the first time.* I assumed that breastfeeding would help me slim down as before. It didn't help. Nothing helped! I left the hospital the very next day after delivering an eight-pound, five-ounce healthy baby girl, weighing nearly the same as when I went in. I was aghast when I realized that, even mortified. Possibly, I was five pounds lighter, yet I needed to buy clothes in a size 14 to 16 after delivery because nothing fit.

In the end, eating what I wanted when I wanted, just *supersized* me like when I went off to college. Only the second pregnancy pushed my cholesterol numbers through the roof on top of the weight gain. The end result was that I was beyond embarrassed with the added weight and stunned by the new cholesterol numbers that emerged (which meant I had to work on that too). The extra pounds wouldn't drop off; they didn't budge one iota. I felt I could starve myself, but no matter what I tried, the scale remained the same. Those were the longest five years ever. Talk about body-image struggles. Then someone had to bully me about my size to top it off, and somebody else had to tell me I looked matronly. Go figure.

Finally, I was clearly fed up and flustered with the added weight, so I saw an endocrinologist just to rule out any abnormality. That's when the doctor informed me I had developed reactive hypoglycemia, and then he proceeded to tell me how to eat for that blood sugar issue. After the visit, I dropped twenty pounds practically overnight, which I hadn't been able to do for the past five years. I was shocked, but in a good sort of way. The only thing I changed was what I ate and when. Sounds simple, right? It wasn't. It took lots of self-control and determination. But for my health, I had to do it. Best of all, I was thrilled with my new size and began to eat better due to mastering the recommended diet, thereby continuing to lose the added weight. In this case, food became medicine.

Still, did my diagnosis occur because I went back to eating sugar, dairy, and wheat products (which contain gluten)? What was the underlying cause? I wasn't sure, but it sure looked like it was what I put inside my mouth because what I had to omit from my diet at that point was sugar and processed foods. The downside was that the initial diagnosis was a preempt leading to a future diagnosis of prediabetes. Between the two disorders, I took another food detour after I started feeling better and paid for it in the future with a prediabetic condition. However, there's another twist in the food journey to health that I didn't see coming. Yet, one day, I would find out more and stick with it.

In reflecting back (way back), a childhood dream of mine was to dance, and when I was young, my mother told me no. That was because she always said, "You're too chubby to be a ballerina." So the years raced forward, and by my mid-thirties I (finally) took ballet and modern dance, which I felt was better late than never. Perhaps one noticeable perk was that ballet helped to trim down my matronly look, as I had been told, and it helped me to whittle away those post-baby pounds, along with sticking to the recommended diet. Plus, I have to add that the criticism on how I looked to someone else wasn't my motivating force. I must clarify that the desire behind the dream to dance fueled my dancing feet. Regardless of my size, looks, or age, the dream became a reality. Incidentally, it's never too late to try something you've always wanted to do. As a nontraditional student, I reached my goal to be *en pointe* in ballet shoes. Hence, the long-lost dream was achieved. That activity lengthened my muscles, thereby strengthening by back, and kept me trim. And I still dance today! My motto has been: I'll dance until I die. There's truly no age discrimination on dance or working out for that matter.

Staying active is one of the keys to longevity. While being bullied for being thin, I've retorted, "I dance (or workout) and eat clean." What could be wrong with those goals? I say this in my own defense. Although I don't owe the naysayers a complex explanation, I find that women quit criticizing me when they hear I dance or workout. Perhaps the former is due to dancers being stereotypically thin, and most people accept that as an absolute. Interestingly enough, that reason seems to stop any critical remarks or subtle bullying. Besides, they pinch your bodyfat and take your weight in some dance schools, and some teachers utilize strict weight guidelines, especially for a principal ballerina (which I am not). Did you know they can be this strict? But I see it's changing for the best, as you can see online today.

Just for the record, on the subject of being thin and bullied, over time I've learned to selectively avoid verbal conflicts, just to keep peace. You know, pick and choose your battles. How do I do it? By changing the subject, choosing to bite my tongue, or asking a question. And I also say a prayer and use this verse: "Set a guard, O Lord, over my mouth; keep watch over the door of my lips (Ps. 141:3). I found this verse to be helpful as it creates peace, not war. If it's not worth the battle, keep peace first is another motto of mine. In Romans 14:19, it says, "Therefore let us pursue the things which make for peace and the things by which one may edify another."

Although today I'm not anorexic or bulimic (and never have been), I am also not overweight any longer. Yet I have learned it's what I choose to eat that has changed for the best, and sticking with it is paramount. Eating healthy is another key to longevity. And another way to look at it is to say you are what you eat, which means I'm a biproduct of what I've consumed. Still, others have actually pulled me aside, saying, "You're looking a bit thin," or, "You look way too thin," and have warned me by adding, "Don't get any thinner." And then there is, "You look thinner than last time. Is everything OK?" Well, when I hear those comments, I generally refrain from getting into a lively debate. Furthermore, the delay could have been due to the fact that it wasn't the right time or place to discuss my size. Does that mean we are going to discuss the other person's size too? Would they like me to talk about their size in return? Probably not is my guess. It's not in my nature to counterpunch; it's not entirely beneficial, and it can be counterproductive in the long run. Who wants to take on a critical debate when you are at a special, memorable event? It's more about enjoying the moment, not rudely ruining it. So I deflect the conversation or play it down, and I forgive before it gets bigger. Instead, I turn the other cheek. (See Matthew 5:39.)

Yet most people have no idea what I've had to overcome or give up in order to feel well. Anyway, who wants to know all the little details? So to keep peace, I don't get into a verbal struggle over other people's opinions or perceptions about my size. If the above was an isolated account, it would be easy to dismiss, but it reoccurs. And most likely, because I was bullied in the past for being overweight (on more than one occasion), I have chosen not to invade anyone's space on size issues when individuals have become openly judgmental about my appearance. For many today, the topic of our weight or size remains a sensitive subject to explore among ourselves, let alone try and write about it.

Personally, it's frustrating to be sidelined by people who wear a different size than me. I never would dream of offending anyone in return. I really thought this would end, yet I've been astonished by being bullied for being thin. To top it off, skinny-shaming exists in person and online and is a definable term, as is the term *thin privilege*. Never once did I hear those terms mentioned while growing up, but now you hear them mentioned all the time. Skinny-shaming or thin privilege is just as bad as fat-shaming, and none of it is right or OK. Regardless, all are a form of body-shaming, which is a form of criticizing, belittling, or tearing another person down and, hence bullying. We are not here on earth to tear each other apart or become anyone's target. The Word says in Ephesians 4:29: "Let no corrupt word proceed out of your mouth, but what is good for necessary edification, that it may impart grace to the hearers." In other words, we need to build each other up.

Many years ago, someone pointed out to me her own observation when she shared, "Take into consideration the person who is judging you. They're the ones with the body image problem to solve, and it must bother them, or they wouldn't be projecting it onto you." That person helped me to see it wasn't my problem to fix. It wasn't my mouth being critical, judgmental, or rude or giving *that look,* which despairingly disapproves of the way someone appears. In the end, she also added, "They're just jealous." Again, I will never understand jealousy. When someone bullies me for being thin, I don't resort to these replies: "Well, look at you. … You should try eating right. It might just help." Or, "Maybe you should exercise. Just look in the mirror." If I should say these statements, the person might conclude that I'm the bully. And, once more, this does not edify or build another person up. Still, why say anything close to these statements if it isn't encouraging? Life is short. Having been there myself, I understand how they may feel, so I watch what I say and say nothing derogatory, demeaning, or offensive. It's not my position to tear someone else down.

What would you tell someone who bullies a person of a different size? How would you handle it? Avoid the conflict (easiest to do), address it (somewhat complicated), get in the person's face (not a good idea), or let it go and forgive (somewhat easy, yet necessary)? Then an afterthought to all of this drama could be to switch your thinking, switch the subject, or do both.

Here is another example of being bullied for being thin: Once upon a time, in a faraway place, I joined a club and knew of some people who would schedule a liposuction procedure (which is an elective surgery), only if they put on too much weight. They often laughed while saying to each other which part of their body, they wanted to lipo again. Liposuction is when a body is marked and the visceral fat is literally sucked out of a person. Afterward, you wear a body bandage, and presto, you've lost the added weight quickly. For me, my experience was the opposite, which wasn't a laughing matter in the end. From time to time, one of the club members who was scheduled for surgery, would bully me about my size. Ironically, because of my food choices, my weight remained consistent, and theirs vacillated for whatever reason. That led to a concern over my weight. I wasn't concerned; they were concerned for me. When that happened, the spokesperson for that small group decided to confront me in private about how thin I appeared to them, as I was being gossiped about behind my back. Surprisingly, that conflict occurred more than once, and I was in a good frame of mind each time (until the discussion). Go figure. So being courteous and to deescalate a recurring situation, my answer became the truth, "I had to quit eating sugar, dairy, and gluten for health reasons. When I changed my diet, I felt better, and my weight stopped fluctuating up and down on the scale." And out of respect to that situation, what more could I say? I couldn't go there. I couldn't enter a verbal power struggle over my size. Besides, it was not in my best interest in the long run.

Furthermore, they were unaware that I had been rebuilding my health, and instead of showing any kind of compassion or understanding, they passed judgment based on their opinions and not facts. What more could I add? Being cordial, I never shared what I really thought of the private inquisition, deciding not to argue and take the high road instead. What I actually wanted to say (and yet I wasn't in the position to say) was, "Why are you pulling me aside and harassing me in private about my weight when you don't really know me? Yet you turn around and have surgery so that you can eat whatever you want. I can't do that." For real, I didn't know this individual, and I didn't want to instigate an argument over our weight differences, body perceptions, exercise routines, or lack thereof. I wouldn't say anything to stir up strife. So in return, I deflated the conversation, held my tongue in check, kept my mouth closed, and walked away. Still, I forgave and continued on about the day.

Of interest is this verse in Proverbs 20:3: "It is an honor for a man to cease from strife: but every fool will be meddling" (KJV). Squabbling and meddling only serve to escalate a stressful state of affairs between others. My point is that I know overweight people get bullied, which is not fair or right, I've been there while growing up, as you have read, but I also know thin people get bullied for being fit and trim, which is not fair or right either. This is why I wrote about both sides. I couldn't believe that type of subtle bullying or covert bullying could happen until I experienced it for myself. Body-shaming in either direction is not fair or right for anyone. And most of all, it's a forgivable offense.

Now, a similar scenario played out, adding to the private insults over my size. An acquaintance I wasn't close to and hardly knew spoke of her weight gain. She confided that she was overweight in passing but also admitted that she bought new clothes due to the extra weight. After her confession, she had the audacity to open her mouth and scold me for being thin. And she wasn't joking. Where was that coming from? At first, I was actually in a good mood and engaged in listening to her up until that point. It was such an awkward moment with another conflict over size taking place in private, and I was totally caught off guard. Yet I smiled at her insults and changed the subject to avoid any arguments over our size differences. Again, I was in a social situation where an open conflict would not be advised. Certainly, I didn't discuss her appearance and didn't retaliate over the offense. Where would that lead our conversation? I don't think she would have appreciated me opening my big mouth in return, recalling our situation. Without much hesitation, I let it go. That was hard, but I let it go anyway. Likewise, with her abrupt conduct (which I wasn't happy about), I kept peace between us, forgiving her unnecessary offense (like I wanted to be offended over my size once more). Yet our acquaintanceship was winding down, and that had nothing to do with size.

Here's one last twist over size: It was time for my annual medical exams, and I had scheduled two different appointments for the same week. On my first visit, the doctor took one look at me and told me, "You look underweight." Well, I gulped and then I thought, *Here we go again. Go figure.* Of course, I didn't say anything counterproductive because I was thinking about what the doctor had previously said to me on our last visit. In conclusion, my doctor requested some routine lab tests, and for a split second, I glanced down at the doctor's notes and then saw these words: "Patient is underweight." That seriously bugged me, but again, I smiled my fake smile and thought, *Isn't this odd. Only last year the (same) doctor said, "You look wonderful."* Imagine that. And I weighed the same as before. So was it the outfit? I'm just guessing. …

However, during my second appointment of the week, I experienced the complete opposite review. Ironically, that doctor entered the room where I'd been waiting and informed me, "You look great!" Plus, she admired my outfit—no kidding. What an added bonus to hear alongside of a wonderful conversation. It made my week! At the close of my last appointment, the doctor found me free and clear of any health concerns right then, and after the results of the CBC (complete blood count) were reviewed, I found even my cholesterol had come down. Certainly, all of it was great news.

So, after living through many changes, some good some not, that was awesome news for my ears to hear, especially after overcoming several health concerns. Yet, in the end, whose report would you believe? Furthermore, they both saw my outward appearance from a completely different point of view—their own. What a parallel those two back-to-back appointments and *opinions* prove concerning someone judging by appearance and not having all the facts. Yet, overall, I believe my health report spoke for itself. I'm so grateful for a good report.

YOU ARE WHAT YOU EAT

Now for the grand finale, I'll discuss being bullied for eating healthy. Who does this? Coincidentally, that has happened right in front of me when people who are eating highly processed and artificially sweetened foods frown down on me for not participating. Besides, they certainly can eat whatever they choose, and I will not oppose them. Yet there are others who have criticized me for eating organically grown foods and less meat in the quest for health. Remarkably, it occurs. This has improved over the years due to the growing health concerns of GMOs, pesticides, fake food additives, and Frankenfoods, which are lab-created foods. These concerns have gained national attention and blame for wreaking havoc on our bodies. And absolutely, people have become more aware and concerned over what is placed in their food.

However, I've been ridiculed by people who will not research for themselves or listen to news reports stating the truth about what is in their food. Yet they feel they have the right to be demeaning or disrespectful when I am trying try to eat real food without the added bioengineered chemicals and preservatives that made me ill. This has also been defined as eating clean and green. Honestly, I don't look for people's opinions on my dietary restrictions. It's quite the contrary. Their opinions are offered freely for my hearing. Even if I try to justify or explain my food choices or past health issues (which I've overcome through prayer and by eating healthy), I'm left asking this prevailing question: Why shame me for being different? Most people can change their diets if they want to, but regardless, I had to change mine, and it had a wonderful impact on my health. Besides, their diets are not up to me to fix, even if I believe they are unhealthy. They would have to want to make the changes themselves. So on occasion, I get to hear subtle digs about my healthy food choices when I'm trying to enjoy a meal, eat right, and stay informed versus getting sick. And who really wants to be sick?

Personally, I'm just trying to enjoy a meal at a social gathering without the added bickering going on. I never intend to argue over what I'm eating. I don't harass other people for what is on their plates. Besides, I'm there to enjoy the company of others and to eat a wonderful meal together. It never ceases to amaze me that the private jabs seem to ruin my attitude. Well, forgiveness extended. Again, that experience has not been an isolated case, or it would be by far the easiest to dismiss and get over.

A book to read that I found helpful on staying healthy was Dr. Caroline Leaf's *Think and Eat Yourself Smart*. Her book, as well as other books, have helped me to stay the course on my quest for a clean bill of health versus the sugar blues. Who can find fault with such a goal? In any case, I've learned to shrug it off and pick and choose my battles, giving up on some entirely to keep peace. In James 3:2, it says, "For in many things we offend all. If any man offends not in word, the same is a perfect man, and able also to bridle the whole body." Knowing offenses do come, I try to walk in forgiveness instead of holding onto any grudge. This has proven over and over again to be an ideal way for me to react in a public setting. Perhaps knowing when and how to bow out of a dispute that is not worth the time or effort is at best an acquired artform. There are bigger fish to fry, as the saying goes, than one woman's diet.

Yet, while we're here, let me expound. I needed to change my food choices, not by fad but by experimentation because I grew tired of being sick and tired, which I have said before. To experiment, I eliminated gluten. Prior to that food elimination, I had tried other restrictive diets in order to feel well. Gradually, I eliminated *white* products—no white sugar, no white salt, no white flour, and no dairy. Except for when I took a few detours on my journey to becoming healthy, wherein I would revisit those forbidden foods and then pay for it later by not feeling well. Why no white products? Well, these products in their raw, original state are not white. Think about it. They are chemically altered, sad to say. Years ago, I often said, "Stay away from processed white foods and processed foods in general," which was ahead of the curve. It's more accepted now than ever before due to a wide array of books and online research. However, in the late seventies and early eighties, that was not always the case. It was quite the opposite. ...

My goal in the early eighties was to be a vegetarian, and I did see some health improvements until I fell off the wagon in keeping that goal and took a food detour instead. Additionally, that particular diet was highly frowned upon back then, but I gave it a try to see if I would feel better on less. Anyhow, I endured being publicly shunned by some friends in a group over food because I refrained from eating processed foods or out at certain fast-food chain restaurants like they were accustomed to. To top that off, the individual who sparked the comments held no credentials on the subject, giving me advice without any facts. On the other hand, yes, I did and do eat out, and there are definitely more food choices available at restaurants today than ever before, which is wonderful. Besides that, I was on my way to wellness by eliminating the above foods at the time, meaning, I began to see progress as I pioneered healthy ways of eating in order to feel better. It just meant going against the grain and adhering to what worked.

Eventually, what came to fruition was the Mediterranean diet minus the dairy. Add to this plan low-glycemic vegetables, fruits with anti-inflammatory properties, and gluten-free whole grains. Plus, these fats are also included: olive oil, flaxseed meal, nuts, and seeds. As much as possible, I try to eat all organic in order to stay away from antibiotics, pesticides, and herbicides. Travel and visiting others can present a challenge, but I've learned to adjust my food choices and bring edibles with me or something to share. This food lifestyle evolved over time, as you can read. And occasionally, I will eat organic chicken or seafood. However, my portions are small to very small, with larger amounts of plant-based proteins such as beans, legumes, nuts, seeds, and peanut butter (which is a legume). I must also add that I prefer seafood over chicken, but due to the toxins in some seafoods, I get to see seafood more than I get to enjoy it. And it's hard to leave out chocolate altogether, so I do savor a piece (or two or three) of dark organic chocolate or gluten-free, black bean chocolate brownies from time to time. Then there is my fall favorite: a velvety vegan pumpkin pie without the added sugar. And yes, there is a great recipe for this yummy pie too on the internet. Well, there you have it in a nutshell (pun intended).

Today, some have linked the above diet to being a flexitarian, which means you are primarily a vegetarian but sometimes eat fish or meat as in the Mediterranean diet. They both appear to overlap each other. Either way, this has been my mainstay diet based on years of trial, error, and research just to feel well and overcome prior health obstacles that I was once diagnosed with. No one really knew the full story on why I had to change, yet they bullied me for being different.

When it comes to being gluten-free, I hardly knew what that term meant years ago, and I didn't know it is an allergen. Was that the missing element to my wellness in the past? I had to find out, and I set out to figure it out. Since I was a child, I fought stomach ailments and couldn't get to the root cause. Once when I was little, my mother took me to a doctor to have my stomach checked. Because food allergies and diagnostics were not part of his protocol, the doctor conducted an X-ray instead, and having seen nothing irregular, he sent us on our way to purchase over-the-counter remedies. For years (and years) those were my go-to medicines. Then came the natural remedies, including herbs, and I tried all of those as well to no avail. I will add that I found relief in some of them but not the cure I was searching for. The discomfort in my stomach felt like a lifetime gone awry until my experiment with gluten. I've written in journals throughout the years that after digesting pizza, pasta, cereals, breads, or desserts, I would become ill and not know why. I thought the culprit was the sugar only or the dairy and sugar, but that was not the entire picture.

Privately, I battled chronic fatigue, stomach nausea or irritation, cramps, and bloating with overall weakness and malaise most of my life. Later, I attributed the problems to reactive hypoglycemia after the endocrinologist gave me the diagnosis and then much later to prediabetes. I could not quite put my finger on it, as something was missing. Even in old journals that I saved I had written, "I just ate pancakes and became sick," or "I just ate pizza and fell ill." I never realized it was the flour; I only suspected the sugar. That went on and on for years when I tried to eat as most other people ate and could not. Organic wheat products were included in what bothered me, as I would later find out.

At some point, I realized the answer was underneath my nose. I couldn't eat the standard American diet, or SAD. It was clearly making me sick and frustrated as time went on. Eventually, I developed and battled chronic dermatitis for nearly a decade and visited many dermatologists that gave me prescriptions and topical medicines to combat the itchy rashes. I also suffered bouts of cystic acne periodically, which left pockmarks, hyperpigmentation, and scars on my face. I was prescribed an array of antibiotics to combat the acute acne and chemical peels to correct the damage left behind. The peels I didn't mind so much, as they have some antiaging benefits. That was more or less a perk for experiencing the treatment, and of course, I didn't mind the benefits. But that is what went on behind the scenes, while in person it was quite another story.

So, on a whim and out of sheer exasperation one day, I mentioned to one of the girls at the local organic grocery store my dilemma. However, when that kind person heard my chief list of ailments, she replied, "Have you ever thought of eliminating gluten?"

My reply back to her was, "Seriously? What is gluten?"

She informed me, "Many people are gluten sensitive, allergic to gluten, or have celiac disease. All you have to do is stay away from products containing gluten. Gluten is in wheat, rye, barley, spelt, triticale, and oats."

When I heard the news, it sounded like an easy fix, although I wished I had heard about it sooner. In return, I told her, "I will definitely give this a try, as I've tried just about everything else out there besides eliminating certain foods." At that point, I was beyond desperate to find an answer in order to feel well and willing to try something new to get there. Yet that fix sounded way too simple. Well, was it also the missing piece of information I had been searching for all those years?

Bravo! I'm glad I gave the experiment of omitting gluten a try. What a huge success it has been, and it was free for the doing. It's called an elimination diet. I just didn't know about getting rid of gluten as part of the elimination process. My only regret is I wish I had known about it sooner— years sooner. Possibly, gluten intolerance was hidden from the public? It certainly did not pop up in anything I had read in the past, at least before the internet. Although many books have surfaced in recent years, it has now turned into a debatable subject online. Nonetheless, that insight has been a real game changer for me physically, and the proof was in the omission. My dermatitis is completely healed. The bloating and stomach problems have pretty much vanished. The chronic fatigue, weakness, and malaise have lifted. The hypoglycemia is long gone, along with the prediabetes. My health was restored due to simple dietary changes, lots of prayer for direction, and aerobics. After that physical victory, I just had to return to the health food store and visit the person who gave me that small piece of advice. It was to thank her from the bottom of my heart for changing my life by avoiding gluten. Once it was said by Hippocrates: "Let food be thy medicine and medicine be thy food." And that medicine in food worked for me.

To make a long journey shorter, the campaign for health appears easy, but it has not always been the case, as you have read. From the time I turned seventeen and gave up drugs, I searched throughout the years ways to feel well, to eat this and not that, to read and try new diets, or to eliminate certain foods until something worked and a breakthrough came. Yet subtle bullying existed even when I was trying to get better. Whether it came through critical or judgmental statements, ridicule, or even the disgruntled awkward look at what I was eating. Sometimes there were outright sighs from others as to why I eat what I eat when asked and even verbal accusations for not eating like them. Maybe you have experienced this too on your quest to feel well. Regardless of the offense, forgiveness is key.

Still, they remain the nameless, faceless people who we may or may not know who have so much to say on how we do life. In the end, keep the good, and let go of the not so good. And just know that people are not always aware of what goes on behind the scenes. Explanation or no explanation, I could not always divulge my case history of what I have overcome except to say, "I have shared some of my struggles and overcoming victories here." Today, eating clean and green has become totally accepted, embraced, and understood as a whole food lifestyle. This lifestyle was not well accepted in the seventies or eighties, but the pioneers of real food have watched it flourish throughout the years through research, discovery, and education. Perhaps it was born out of a need for change in one's health status, a desire for longevity, or a need for healing. Maybe some have become sick and tired of being sick and tired and have decided to pursue a different way of eating, including me. Sometimes, this is the impetus needed before change can take place. Overall, let's each take care of the one body God gave us. Why bully over food that others are eating to become or to stay healthy? Instead, let us appreciate and enjoy each other with our unique differences as we continue forward on our journeys. From body image to the foods we eat, and everything in between, know that Christ is working inside each one of us to do His good pleasure as we try to shape our lives after Him.

IN CONCLUSION

The biggest claim I could add to sum up "Fit, Thin, and Bullied" is, thankfully, I'm healthier today than I've ever been in the past. I have won many physical victories while facing health obstacles (diseases) that no one knew about. Truthfully, I did not even name a few of them. Over my lifetime, I have experienced instantaneous healings and miracles, as well as those that required me to change, which promoted healing as in this story. My health was restored in part because I underwent a dietary transformation and stuck with it after living through several detours along the way. What a difference the right foods can make on the journey. The art of self-discipline brought wellness and healing. Even though I know God can heal instantly, in this case, it took time to overcome. Besides, it was important to forgive others over the words they spoke in regard to my size or appearance, for what I ate or did not eat, for my diet, or for being different.

Last of all, I give all the glory to God for being healed and restored. "For in Him we live and move and have our being" (Acts 17:28).

Now, to anyone who has suffered privately or in front of others over any type of body-shaming, diet, being different, or whatever the case may be, know that the Lord can fully heal and restore you from anything you have endured, creating a new you going forward.

In using the Keys to Forgiveness Scale of one through ten, I am giving this chapter a two and some events a four. Those subtle or moderate bullying offenses (which are also described in the introduction) were by far the easiest to forgive and get over, as you can read in Appendix I and in "Solutions for Overcoming" in Appendix II.

IN LOOKING BACK

Although we don't always have the power to change every unpleasant circumstance in our lives, we do have the power to change our outlook.

— Joyce Meyer Ministries

In looking back, this entire book project was not only a process but a journey to a destination. I never dreamt of where this book would lead me, fueled by the realization that a great quantity of the original outline dealt with the bully drugs and the culture that goes with it. Apart from acknowledging traumatic events that happened to me behind the scenes, I know I'm not the only one. I wrote with this in mind. To top it off, this book mirrors the fact that addiction and abuse has touched everyone's life in one way or the other, hurting everyone involved on some level. In some way an epidemic has infiltrated a nation, and that fact is hard to escape and certainly harder to ignore when drugs or abuse hit close to home and you can't ignore it. Or maybe it was you (like me) at one time, the old nature, the old self, *or the prodigal,* which we've put off and gotten rid of. Or possibly it was you at one time (like me too) where we've experienced abuse outside of our control, yet we walked away alive but on our way to recovery. And all to the glory of God, we survived. With this in mind, I wrote.

At first, I reminisced, *This book should be about the extreme makeover that took place in my life. Going from being bullied for being overweight as a child to bullied for being thin as an adult.* But that wasn't it. Next, I considered, *This book should be about nutrition and diet. Taking what I used to eat as a food addict and comparing it to everything I eat today. It would also include research and nutritional discoveries.* But that wasn't it either. It also wasn't about the mean girls, the male bullies, or dating. However, those memories definitely played a part or held a chapter inside this book.

There again, I went on thinking, *If this book could help anyone to know that bad things happen to good people, you just need to get through it in order to get to the other side, well then, I would like to share.* But I knew that wasn't my purpose-driven mission; consequently, I discarded the concept and then reconsidered. This contemplative search led me right back to the beginning. As I said in the first chapter, I did not plan to share my personal testimony on salvation and deliverance from drug abuse as a teen and as a prodigal child, but when I did open up and link this story to the other stories, I saw a pattern emerge outside of myself. It was watching others ravaged by drugs and bullied by heroin, a soaring national epidemic, with millions of people trying to deal with it. And the hardest part was seeing and hearing about other people who have died in their drug-induced addiction or to hear of others involved with an addict continuously in and out of rehab but still hoping for the addict to become free from the hold drugs have had on his or her life and mind.

Then it took bravery to revisit both the molestation and the rape from my youth. Yet what inspired this were the untold stories from others now immerging, including mine. I am silent no more because my heart goes out to those who cannot tell their stories but need or want help or a solution. It's heart-wrenching to say the least, these true-life stories. For some, it becomes a storm to persevere through and manage. For others, it turns into a dark nightmare to get out of. All you know is that you wish the horrible dream would go away and it doesn't, at least not right away. To some degree, this was the motivation behind the book too, but it was more about knowing Jesus is the answer to help calm the storm or to carry you through the storm, and He is the way out of any storm that life may bring. And then, times of refreshing can come from above. Healing and restoration can come, and a new beginning can unfold.

With all of this in mind, you get to see the challenges created by bullies, abuse, and addicts unwind. Whether anyone wants to or not, I, you, we, or others cannot ignore this universal tragedy of people hurting people needlessly. Perhaps, they are souls in need of a Savior or in need of deliverance and in need of forgiveness.

Yet, while I was working on the content for this book, I couldn't just write about the trauma I endured without a solution. More important was that tragedy was followed by forgiveness, leading to overcoming through Jesus Christ. He is the reason why I'm alive today. So many times, I could have been dead (even though I had felt mostly dead inside) or should have been dead but wasn't. God had His hand on my life. I know I'm a miracle today, and He is a miracle-working God, working among us and in us and through us. "And they overcame him by the blood of the Lamb and by the word of their testimony" (Rev. 12:11). In other words, Jesus will empower us to overcome any tragedy, thereby giving us victory and a new testimony to share of His goodness.

Given the pursuit to understand the drug culture past or present, to watch others on heroin, to know of other Christians using in secret, besides the many faces of abuse, led me to come full circle on my quest to finish this book. And I knew I could not deny these stories. I couldn't just shut my eyes to them, tune them out, or pretend they didn't happen. They certainly became part of the book on this journey called life, not to mention the resolve of inner healing and restoration, which is so needed today in the world we live in and can be wrapped up in this verse: "I would have lost heart, unless I had believed that I would see the goodness of the Lord in the land of the living" (Ps. 27:13). And this too, His goodness, was important to share, along with other key verses. All of it (the good, the bad, and the ugly) combined inside this book blends into having a grateful heart and knowing there is a God who wants to heal, deliver, and restore the tragic, broken places that we have walked through. No matter what we have experienced, God's love is omnipresent and unfathomable and merciful. This is God loving people right where they are *unconditionally.*

In looking back, I would have never intentionally set out to cover the topic of drugs as compared to other timely topics. But there was the answer staring me in the face, making it hard to shove aside once I saw my testimony in print. And believe me, I wanted to ignore it and paint a pretty picture instead—that I lived a perfect life in a perfect world, but that is not what happened to me while growing up. Anything short of reality would be a mirage or a facade. This book chronicles from the beginning to the end stages of an addict and abuse and more. ... Yet the stories have different outcomes, as you have read. Honestly, I wish each chapter had ended on a positive note, but the truth remains. Life can be messy at times and short, it's not a perfect science, it can become complicated, and, well, life doesn't always play fair, as in some of these stories. It's what you do with what you know that counts and whom you turn to.

Above all, the best part with everything and anything that we have ever had to face or walk through is to know Christ. That really counts at the end of the day—at the end of one's life. In 2 Corinthians 2:14, it reads, "Now thanks be to God who always leads us in triumph in Christ, and through us diffuses the fragrance of His knowledge in every place." There is victory over what we've gone though, and the Lord gives "beauty for ashes," as it says in Isaiah 61:3. Plus, I just had to add beauty for ashes, because that has been me many times over being refashioned, but the promise applies to you as well.

At "The End," the final end of this book, I know and believe that the Lord wants to heal all of our brokenness inside and out from our past and even our present, bringing us abundant life—you know, the things out of our control, the mistakes we have made, or the bullying, abuse, or any type of addiction. Know that the Lord has a destiny, a purpose, and a plan for our lives to apprehend. It's never too late for a new beginning. Finally, let us in faith take our needs to the Lord because He is our sovereign Savior Who heals and restores. We are a work—His work—in progress, and He promises to continue to work in us until the day of His coming again.

> Then I went down to the potter's house, and there he was, making something at the wheel. And the vessel that he made of clay was marred in the hand of the potter; so, he made it again into another vessel, as it seemed good to the potter to make. (Jer. 18:2–4)

The Lord is the potter, and we are the clay. Transform us into a new vessel to be used by You today.

THE KEYS TO FORGIVENESS SCALE (KFS)

Objective and purpose: Why a scale? The scale was born out of a need to overcome and let whatever go forever. Some experiences were easy to quickly get over. Others, even though I forgave, felt as if they were taking forever to get over. Possibly, it was due to the trauma that was attached to the experience or because in the past resources were not readily available. However, to use the scale for yourself, you must first acknowledge the level of bullying or abuse by choosing a category, along with the effect it has had on your life on a scale of one to ten.

This system validates the event and the severity of it as you let go of it for good. It may help you understand why some situations are easier or harder to forgive and get over compared to others. Following your selection, forgive and release the event and the individual or people involved, and rerelease if necessary. The objective is to let go. Let the person, people, or group go in your head and heart. And some may need to physically let go of someone or something. Let the offense, injustice, trauma, or pain of it all go. Ask the Lord to dig deep inside of you, and let Him take it all out. Nothing is too hard for the Lord to do. The purpose: forgiveness leads to healing, and healing brings restoration to your mind, body, and soul. For examples to see, I have personally used and included this scale throughout the book.

Directions: Identify the number related to the category your experience best fits. Then forgive and give it all to God in prayer, moving forward and letting go of the past for good.

KEYS TO FORGIVENESS SCALE

1–2 = Borderline to Minimal: Easiest to forgive and move forward quickly. (No big deal.)

3–4 = Moderate: Harder to forgive and get over quickly. (I'll forgive and get over it.)

5–7 = Moderate to Acute: Slightly intolerable; challenging to forgive and move forward. (I need grace and will get over it, but I do forgive.)

8–9 = Maximum to Borderline Severe: Intolerable; very challenging to forgive, move forward, and get over. (It may take time and grace to get over, but I choose to forgive.)

10 = Severe to Beyond Severe: Very intolerable; extremely difficult and challenging to forgive and get over. (It may take time, grace, and possibly continued forgiveness, but I will overcome.)

Note: The scale above is designed to validate the depth of the event that occurred in your life. The outcome is the same for each category: forgiveness leading to restoration. May this help you to recapture your life by taking it back bit by bit or all at once.

Forgiveness produces the following:

1. Forgiveness helps to create a clean heart before the Lord. (See Psalms 51:10.)
2. Forgiveness breaks yokes, aids in breakthroughs, opens the door for healing, and brings freedom. (See Isaiah 10:27.)
3. Ask God for the ability to forgive even when it's hard to forgive. (See Matthew 7:7.)
4. You may not "feel" like you forgave at first. Walk away and give it time. It's a choice and act of your will. It's not based on feelings. (See Colossians 3:13.)

5. Forgiveness will affect the posture of your heart. (See 1Samuel 16:7.)
6. If someone repeats an offense, you may need to forgive again. Repeat as often as needed. (See Matthew 18:21–22.)

STRATEGIES FOR OVERCOMING

The following keys and tips are life skills that have helped me overcome, and I have practiced them throughout my life as needed. Many times, they took me from victim to survivor to overcomer, thereby bringing healing and restoration. In the same way, may they bless and encourage you in your walk.

1. Read the Bible: Look up verses that pertain to your situation. Post promises and uplifting scriptures in your home. Speak the Word over your circumstances and life.
2. Pray and prayer support: Seek the Lord. Ask Him for healing. Confide in a prayer team or trusted individual.
3. Play music, sing, and worship: Play uplifting music, and sing through the storms in life. Worship the Lord in song, therefore changing the atmosphere around you.
4. For sleep, try one of the following: Pray, give thanks, or play soothing worship music in the background. Also, quote and meditate on memory verses from the Bible instead of dwelling on the trauma.
5. Develop a network of support: Seek out friends, family, church groups, or special interest groups.
6. Develop an action plan: Go through the adversity if it cannot be avoided. Remind yourself that this too shall pass. In advance of any special holiday, dates, or upcoming event, have a plan and work your plan.

7. Post positive statements: Place verses, quotes, affirmations, or sayings, where you can see them. Read Christian books that are positive and encouraging. They will edify, affirm, and build you up.

8. Make appointments: See a trusted counselor, pastor, or friend. Seek out positive role models or mentors.

9. Implement a strategy: Try using the buddy system if and when needed.

10. Make use of a plan: Understand yell and tell. Develop a workable plan for your protection. Know and understand boundaries.

11. Journal privately: Let it all out in writing, and then give it to the Lord.

12. Refrain and refuse to use: Don't use any word or phrase that tears you down, which may lead to self-hatred.

13. Retrain and reframe your thought patterns: Refuse to stay stuck in old thoughts and memories after you have dealt with a situation. Take captive negative, imbedded thoughts or labels that have been placed on you. Then, replace them with positive self-talk and how the Lord sees you. Make a list of statements and/or verses and review. Give the labels, recurring thoughts or memories, or what people have said to you or about you to the Lord.

14. Address emotions: Find constructive ways to let out your emotions, not destructive ones. Reconstruct your attitude. Reinvent yourself. It's never too late for positive change.

15. Find your focus: Remain focused and focus forward. Do the next thing or create a list to do. Focus on the good. Aim for progress both upward and outward.

16. Regain or maintain health: Exercise for health and to release any negative emotions. Develop a workout plan for stress. Eat for health to combat stress and to fight disorders or any disease. Create doable goals for yourself.

17. Do a self-checkup: Make sure you take care of yourself, and schedule something you'll look forward to. Do something nice for yourself or for someone else.

18. Avoid toxic people: If you can stay away from toxic people and situations, do. If impossible, take the toxicity in small doses if you cannot avoid the person or people and situation.
19. Let go: You may need to physically let go of someone or something or a habit that is causing you harm.
20. Reach out: When possible, pay it forward and touch another life!

Yet in all these things we are more than conquerors through Him who loved us.

— Romans 8:37

ABOUT THE AUTHOR

For a fact, this author knows that what was meant for evil, God can turn it around for good! While in college, doors opened for Grace Francis to work with troubled teens in the social services field. Not only did she work in treatment facilities, but she managed a group home where she worked closely with juveniles from the court, drug addicts, and abused children. Her heartbeat was to aid in their recovery and to demonstrate unconditional love. If she could make a difference, it was to help them overcome.

The desire to change lives brought Grace to a public platform within the church through the performing arts. This powerful medium of expression included traveling with a Christian theater troupe to campuses and churches, whereby she shared her testimony of a life transformed by the power of Christ.

In time, a new season opened doors for Grace as a licensed advanced aesthetician, makeup artist, and CPCP in clinical aesthetics while working as an educator, consultant, and manager. It was during this season of touching faces and touching lives that no one really knew what truly was going on behind the scenes. Through introspection and reflection, she saw a need to write about bullies, abuse, and addiction. With the former in mind, Grace hopes to portray that a heart of forgiveness is a pathway to healing and restoration.

You can connect with Grace at
www.gracetorestore.com

Printed in the USA
CPSIA information can be obtained
at www.ICGtesting.com
LVHW041618170923
758449LV00042B/581

9 781664 226753